SUBSTITUTES FOR FLESH FOODS

Vegetarian
Cook
Book

By E. G. FULTON

Creative Cook Books
Monterey, California

Vegetarian Cook Book

by
E. G. Fulton

ISBN 1-58963-074-2

Reprinted from the 1904 edition

Creative Cookbooks
An imprint of Fredonia Books
Monterey, California
http://www.creativecookbooks.com

WHY I WAS IMPRESSED TO WRITE A COOK BOOK.

It must appeal to the judgment of every thinking man and woman that the human family are more in need of sound, wholesome advice as to what they should eat and drink than ever before. The number of physicians and dentists increases each year at an alarming rate, but the aches and ills of the suffering people do not lessen. Thousands of people find themselves in a deplorable condition, with stomachs almost worn out, having depended largely upon pre-digested foods and a long list of so-called "dyspepsia cures."

The amount of patent medicines, "sure cures," consumed by the people in the United States is enormous, and is increasing every year. It must be apparent to all students of the past century that the people of the present are not enjoying the same degree of health as our ancestors, nor have we any assurance that things will improve unless some radical change is made.

Disease among cattle, poultry, and fish has increased so alarmingly in the last few years that we should no longer depend on the animal kingdom for food. We should look to the grains, nuts, vegetables, and fruits for a better dietary than can be prepared from the flesh of animals likely to be contaminated with tuberculosis, cancer, and other diseases.

In writing this book, the author has treated the subject from the commonly accepted definition of the term vegetarianism, which means to abstain from flesh food, but allows the use of eggs, milk, and its products. After years of experience in conducting vegetarian restaurants in several cities and making a study of the food question, he thinks he can bestow no greater gift upon the people than to place before them a book containing instruction in the preparation of wholesome dishes that will build up in place of tearing down the body.

In this work I do not claim to have reached perfection, nor to have exhausted the category of wholesome preparations and combinations within the domain of vegetarianism. In our efforts to teach how to live without the use of flesh foods, we find we have only begun to discover the inexhaustible resources of the great vegetable kingdom in the boundless wealth of varied hygienic foods.

E. G. F.

CONTENTS

HYGIENE OF COOKING

☀ GOOD COOKING ☀

Good cooking is not the result of accident, a species of good luck, as it were. There is reason in every process; a law governing every chemical change. A course of medical lectures does not make a physician, nor will a collection of choice recipes make a cook. There must be a knowledge of compounding, as well as of compiling; of baking, as well as of mixing; and above all, one must engage in the real doing. Theory alone will not suffice; but experience, which practice only can give, is of the utmost importance.

Mention will be made under this head of those forms of cooking only which enter into vegetarian cooking as usually understood.

BOILING

The term "boiling," as applied to cookery, means cooking in a boiling liquid. Many kinds of food need the action of water or other liquid, combined with heat, to cook them in the best manner, and boiling is one of the most common forms of cookery. When water becomes too hot to bear the hand in it with comfort, it has reached one hundred and fifty degrees, or the scalding point. When there is a gentle tremor or undulation on the surface, one hundred and eighty degrees, or the simmering point, is reached. When there is quite a commotion on the surface of the water, and the bubbles breaking above it throw off steam or watery vapor, two hundred and twelve degrees, or the boiling point, is reached.

After water reaches the boiling point it becomes no hotter, no matter how violently it may boil. The excess of heat escapes in the steam. This important fact is rarely understood by the average cook, and much fuel is often needlessly wasted because of the mistaken idea that rapidly boiling water cooks food more quickly.

In all ordinary cooking, simmering is more effective than violent boiling. The temperature of the water may be slightly raised by covering the kettle. If sugar or salt or anything to increase its density, is added to water, it takes longer for it to boil, but its boiling temperature is higher. This explains why boiling sugar syrup and boiling salt water are hotter than boiling fresh water. Boiling effects partial destruction or removal of organic and mineral impurities found in water, hence the importance of boiling the water where such impurities exist. Boiling also expels all the air and the gases which give fresh water its sparkle and vitality. Therefore, the sooner water is used after it begins to boil, the more satisfactory will be the cooking.

Fresh water should be used when the object is to extract the flavor, or soluble parts, as in soups and broths. Salt water should be used when it is desired to retain the flavor and soluble parts, as in most green vegetables. Cold water draws out the starch of vegetables. Boiling water bursts starch grains, and is absorbed by the swelling starch, and softens the cellulose in cereals and vegetables.

MILK

In cooking some kinds of food, milk is used instead of water. Milk being thicker than water, less of the steam escapes, and it becomes hot sooner than water, adheres to the pan, and burns easily. At its boiling temperature (214 degrees), the casein contained in milk is slightly hardened, and its fat rendered more difficult of digestion. By heating milk in a double boiler, these dangers are avoided. It then only reaches a temperature of 196 degrees, and is called scalded milk. The process is a form of steaming.

STEAMING

Steaming is a process of cooking food over boiling water. It is a very satisfactory and convenient method, without much loss of substance. It takes a longer time than some other ways of cooking, but requires less attention. There are two methods of cooking by steam: (1) In a steamer, which is a covered pan, with perforated bottom. This is placed over boiling water, and the steam carries the heat directly to the food. (2) By means of a double boiler. By this method the heat is conveyed from the boiling water, through the inner boiler to the food. When cooking by steam, the water should boil steadily until the food is done. Watery vegetables are made drier by steaming, and flour mixtures develop a different flavor than when baked.

STEWING

Stewing is cooking in a small quantity of water at

a low temperature for a long time, and is a form of boiling. The food loses less nutriment when stewed than when rapidly boiled.

BAKING

Baking is cooking by means of dry heat, as in a close oven. The closely-confined heat of the oven develops flavors which are entirely different from those obtained by other forms of cooking. The baking of many kinds of food is as important as the mixing, and every cook should thoroughly understand how to regulate the oven. Nearly all flour mixtures, as bread, cakes, and many kinds of pudding, are more wholesome when baked than when cooked in any other way.

BRAIZING

Braizing is a combination of stewing and baking. Meat cooked in a closely-covered stew-pan, so that it retains its own flavor and those of the vegetables and flavorings put with it, is braized. Braized dishes are highly esteemed.

BROILING

Broiling, meaning "to burn," is cooking directly over, or in front of, the clear fire, and is the hottest form of cooking. The intense heat, combined with the free action of the air, produces a fine flavor quite unlike that obtained in any other way. Pan broiling is broiling on a hot surface instead of over hot coals.

SALADS

SALADS

All green vegetables that are eaten raw and dressed with acid, salt, and oil, are included in the list of salads, and they should always be served crisp and cool. Wash salad greens carefully, allowing them to stand in cold or iced water until crisp. Drain and wipe dry with a soft towel, taking care not to bruise the leaves, and keep in cool place till serving time. If they are not thoroughly dried, the water will collect in the bottom of the dish and ruin any dressing used.

Pare cucumbers thickly, and remove a thick slice from each end; cut into thin slices, or into one-half inch dice, and keep in cold water until ready to serve, then drain thoroughly; crisp celery in cold water also.

Pare tomatoes, and keep in a cold place, and sprinkle with chopped ice at serving time. The list of vegetables suitable for salads is so long that the question of kind is wholly a matter of choice. Asparagus, peas, string beans, beets, cauliflower, etc., are all well utilized in salads. Freshly cooked vegetables or left-overs may be used, but all cooked vegetables must be cold and perfectly tender. By deftly combining these left-overs with the favorite dressing, there is material for a delicious and economical salad, to which the somewhat aristocratic name of macedoine salad may be given. This salad may consist of a few or many kinds of vegetables, any com-

(15)

bination pleasing alike to the eye and the palate being permissible, and if care is taken in the arrangement, it may be made a very attractive dish.

To the dressing of salads one must give utmost care and attention, as upon their excellence the success of the dish principally depends. While rules for dressings are innumerable, there are, after all, only a few really good ones. The French dressing and the mayonnaise are most generally known, the former being the simplest and most commonly used of all dressings. And it is quite the favorite for lettuce, cresses, chicory, and other vegetable salads. As the salad wilts if allowed to stand in the dressing, it should not be added till just at the moment of serving, and it is for this reason that it is frequently made at the table.

One of the most difficult things to prepare is a perfect mayonnaise, but once the knack is acquired, failure afterwards is rare. One essential point is to have all the materials cold. Chill in the refrigerator both the bowl and oil an hour or more before using. In warm weather it is advisable during the mixing to stand the bowl in a larger one of cracked ice. This dressing, if covered closely, will keep several days or longer in the ice-box. Keep in a cold place till wanted, as it liquefies as soon as mixed with meat or vegetables. To tone down the taste of the oil, and thus make more delicate salads, one may add to the dressing, just before it is used, a little cream beaten stiff and dry. This dressing is used with

nut and fruit salads, and may be used with potatoes,
tomatoes, celery, and other vegetables.

Most cooked vegetables intended for salads are
moistened with a French dressing and allowed to
stand an hour or more, or until well seasoned, in a
cold place. To this process the term marinate is
applied. Just before serving, pour off all the marinate that is not absorbed, and combine with the
mayonnaise. A mistake frequently made in prepar-
ing salad dressing is that of using too much acid.
The acid flavor should not predominate, but other
flavors should also have their value.

VEGETARIAN CHICKEN SALAD

> Chopped protose, ½ pound.
> Chopped celery, ⅔ cup.
> Grated onion, 1 small teaspoonful.
> Chopped nuttolene, ¼ pound.
> Lemons, juice of 2.
> Salt.
> Mayonnaise, 2 tablespoonfuls.

Mix all together, adding mayonnaise dressing
last. Serve on lettuce.

ALMOND SALAD

> Olives, 18.
> Celery, 1½ cups.
> Blanched almonds, 1½ cups.
> Salad dressing.
> Lettuce.

2

Stone and chop the olives. Add the almonds chopped, also the celery cut fine. Mix with salad dressing and serve on lettuce.

NORMANDIE SALAD

Walnut meats, 1 cup.
French peas, 1 can.
Mayonnaise.
Lettuce.

Place walnut meats in scalding water about fifteen minutes, then remove the skins, and cut into pieces about size of a pea. Scald the French peas, and set aside for a while. Drain the water off the peas, and let them get cold; then mix with the walnuts. Pour mayonnaise dressing over all, and mix thoroughly. Serve on lettuce.

BRAZILIAN SALAD

Ripe strawberries, 1½ cups.
Fresh pineapple, cut in small cubes, 1½ cups.
Brazil nuts, blanched and thinly sliced, 12.
Lemon juice, 4 tablespoonfuls.
Lettuce.
Dressing, 1 spoonful.

Cut the strawberries and pineapples into small cubes, and add thinly-sliced Brazil nuts that have been marinated in lemon juice. Arrange lettuce in rose-shape, and fill the crown with the above mixture, and cover with a spoonful of mayonnaise or golden salad dressing.

NESSLERODE SALAD

Red cherries, ½ cup.
Black cherries, ½ cup.
Red currants, ½ cup.
White currants, ½ cup.
Sugar, 1½ cups.
Red raspberries, ½ cup.
Black raspberries, ½ cup.
Strawberries, ½ cup.
Lemon juice, ½ cup.

Pit the cherries, keeping them as whole as possible. Put a layer of fruit in the salad bowl, then a layer of sugar, then another layer of fruit, and so on, till all the fruit is used, finishing with a layer of sugar. Pour over all one-half cup of lemon juice. Shake the bowl gently from side to side, to draw out the juice until it nearly covers the fruit.

More sugar may be used if needed. This salad should be made two hours before using, and kept on ice.

FRUIT SALAD

Apples, cut in half-inch cubes, 1 cup.
Bananas, cut in half-inch cubes, 1 cup.
Oranges, cut in half-inch cubes, 1 cup.

Mix all together and serve with golden salad dressing.

WALDORF SALAD

Apples, cut in dice, 1½ cups.
Lemon juice, ½ cup.
Lettuce.
Celery, cut in dice, 1½ cups.
Mayonnaise dressing.

Mix apples, celery, and lemon juice well together, and pour mayonnaise dressing over. Serve on lettuce.

In making Waldorf salad use only crisp, white, tart apples, and the tender, white heart of the celery. The celery should be cut a little smaller than the apples. Use only white mayonnaise.

Drain off the lemon juice before adding the dressing, or it will ruin the mayonnaise.

PROTOSE SALAD

Protose, cut in small dice, 1 pound.
Cold, boiled potatoes, cut into dice, 2.
Finely cut celery, ½ cup.
Finely minced onion, 1 tablespoonful.
Salt.
Celery salt, ½ teaspoonful.

Mix thoroughly with mayonnaise, and serve on lettuce leaves.

PROTOSE AND CELERY SALAD

Diced protose, 2½ cups.
Grated onion, 1 tablespoonful.
Oil salad dressing.
Salt, 1 teaspoonful.
Crisp celery, 1¼ cups.
Lettuce or celery leaves.

Cut protose into half-inch dice, add a little salt, grated onion, and celery cut into the same size as protose. Set in ice-box, and just before serving pour over some of the oil salad dressing, and mix all together lightly. Serve on lettuce leaves or garnish with celery leaves.

PEA AND ONION SALAD

Peas, canned or stewed, 4 cups drained.
Grated onion, 2 tablespoonfuls.
Lettuce leaves.
Mayonnaise.

Let peas drain half an hour, then add the onion.
Mix well. Set in a cold place, and when ready to
serve pour over the mayonnaise. Mix all together
lightly, and serve on lettuce leaves.

ENGLISH SALAD

Chopped lettuce, 1 cup.
Chopped celery, 1 cup.
Mayonnaise, 1 tablespoonful.
Lemons, juice of 2.

Mix lettuce, celery, and lemon juice thoroughly,
then add mayonnaise and salt to taste.

WATER LILY SALAD

Lettuce leaves.
Mayonnaise dressing.
Eggs, hard-boiled, 8.

Cut crisp lettuce leaves into pointed strips, like
the outer leaves of a water lily. Cut the whites of
hard-boiled eggs also into strips, to make the petals.
Mash all but two or three of the yolks, mix them
with the mayonnaise, and fill in the center of the
white petals. Take the remaining yolks and put
through a fine sieve, and scatter this over the yellow
center and white petals to resemble pollen of the
flower.

NUT AND FRUIT SALAD

Diced pineapple (canned), 1 cup.
Chopped walnuts, 1½ cups.
Diced oranges, 1 cup.
Diced dates, 1 cup.

Mix all together, and add golden salad dressing one hour before serving.

NUT SALAD

Apple, 1 small.
Lettuce, ½ cup.
Onion juice, 1 teaspoonful.
Oil of cloves, 7 drops.
Salt.
Almonds, ½ cup.
Brazil nuts, ½ cup.
Sugar, 1 teaspoonful.
Lemon, juice of 1.

Chop all the ingredients moderately fine, and mix well with plenty of mayonnaise dressing.

TOMATO MAYONNAISE

Tomatoes, 2.
Oil, ½ cup.
Onion juice, 3 or 4 drops.
Hard-boiled eggs, 2.
Raw egg, 1.

Peel the tomatoes, cut them in halves, and press out all the seeds, retaining only the solid, fleshy portion. Chop this fine; press through a sieve and drain.

Mash very fine the hard-boiled yolks of the eggs,

and add the raw yolk. When thoroughly mixed, add the oil, a few drops at a time. When thick and smooth, add the dry pulp of the tomato, a little at a time. Stir in the onion juice. Serve on sliced protose or nuttolene.

LIMA BEAN SALAD

Lima beans, 2 cups.
Strained tomatoes, 1¾ cups.
Hard-boiled yolks, 2.
Lettuce.
Nut butter, 2 tablespoonfuls.
Minced parsley, 1 tablespoonful.
Salt.
Sliced tomatoes.

Cook beans till well done, strain off the water, and set aside to cool. Mix nut butter as for table use, and thin it down with the tomato juice. Add the minced parsley and a little salt; turn this mixture on the beans, and stir well without breaking the beans. Mince the yolks of the hard-boiled eggs and sprinkle over the salad. Garnish with lettuce and sliced tomatoes, and serve.

PEA AND TOMATO SALAD

Tomatoes, 6.
Nuttolene, 1 cup.
Salad dressing.
Green peas, 2 cups.
Lettuce.

Peel the tomatoes and scoop out the inside. Fill up with green peas and bits of nuttolene. Place each tomato on a lettuce leaf, and cover with salad dressing.

LETTUCE

Separate the leaves and carefully wash to remove every particle of grit. Shake the water off the leaves. Place on a plate or in a salad dish, and send to the table for each to prepare as preferred.

Dress with lemon, salt, or olive oil. A mayonnaise or lettuce dressing may be provided for the table. If preferred, lettuce may be cut fine before being sent to the table.

CABBAGE SALAD

Cabbage chopped very fine, 1½ cups.
Chopped walnuts, ½ cup.
Cream, ½ cup.
Lemon, juice of 1.
Sugar, 1 tablespoonful.
Salt.

Beat cream, sugar, and lemon juice together; then pour over the walnuts, cabbage, and salt, which have been thoroughly mixed.

SALAD LA BLANCHE

Lima beans, 1 cup.
Minced celery, 1 cup.
Hard-boiled eggs, 2.
Minced lettuce, 1 cup.
Nuttolene, ¼ pound.

Boil the beans till tender, drain, and cool. Chop them rather fine, and add the minced celery, minced lettuce, nuttolene cut into small dice, and hard-boiled eggs finely chopped. Serve with La Blanche dressing.

BEET SALAD

Cold, boiled beets.
Hard-boiled eggs.
Salt, olive oil, lemon juice.
Lettuce.

Arrange alternately slices of cold, boiled beet with slices of hard-boiled eggs on a plate. Season with salt, olive oil, and lemon juice poured over. Serve on lettuce.

CARROT AND BEET SALAD

Carrots, 2.
Lettuce.
Dressing.
Beets, 2.
Celery.

Arrange alternately slices of cold, boiled carrots and beets. Serve on a lettuce leaf, garnish with finely-chopped celery.

Dress with olive oil, lemon juice, or French salad dressing.

STUFFED BEET SALAD

Boil the beets whole till tender, selecting those of uniform size. Cut a slice off the bottom, so that they will stand upright, and scoop the inside out carefully. Take pains not only to avoid breaking the shell, but to keep the inside as nearly whole as possible. Peel the shells, and let them get perfectly cold. Cut the centers into tiny cubes, using an equal amount of parboiled potatoes and white celery cut to same size; mix well with mayonnaise or French dressing, and fill the shells, laying a slice of hard-boiled egg on top of each, and serving on a bed of tender lettuce leaves.

TURNIP AND BEET SALAD

Turnips, 1¼ cups.
Green peas, 2 cups.
Mayonnaise.
Beets, 1¼ cups.
Lettuce.

Cook both vegetables separately till tender; dice and set on ice, until ready to serve. Place a spoonful of the mixed vegetables on a leaf of lettuce, border with green peas, and put a spoonful of mayonnaise on top.

ASPARAGUS AND PROTOSE SALAD

Asparagus, 1½ cups.
Protose, 1½ cups.
Salt.
Mayonnaise.

Wash the asparagus and cut into pieces half an inch long. Boil in salted water till tender. Drain off the water, and when cold put into salad dish with protose cut into dice. Season with salt. Serve on a lettuce leaf with mayonnaise.

BEET AND POTATO SALAD

Cut with a vegetable cutter or slice cooked beets and potatoes; arrange on a dish alternately, dress with cream salad dressing.

BEET AND POTATO SALAD NO. 2

Beets, 1 cup.
Protose, ½ cup.
Onion juice, 2 tablespoonfuls.
Hard-boiled egg sliced, 1.
Mayonnaise.
Potatoes, 1 cup.
Egg yolks, ½ cup.
Salt.
Chopped parsley, ¼ cup.
Lettuce.

Cut the beets, potatoes, and protose into small dice. Mix all together and serve on a lettuce leaf; one slice of egg to each portion.

ASPARAGUS AND CAULIFLOWER SALAD

Asparagus tips, boiled and drained, 2 cups.
Cauliflower, boiled, drained, cut in small pieces, 2 cups.

Dress with cream salad dressing.

ASPARAGUS SALAD

Cut cooked asparagus tips into three-inch lengths, and serve on lettuce leaf with cream dressing.

BRUSSELS SPROUTS SALAD

Put plain boiled Brussels sprouts into the ice-chest to get cold. Dress with olive oil and lemon juice. Serve on lettuce.

DATE AND CELERY SALAD

Chop dates and celery, and serve wtih golden salad dressing.

MACEDOINE SALAD

This is a mixture of any kind of cooked vegetables. Cover with French salad dressing, and serve on lettuce leaves.

SALAD DRESSINGS

MAYONNAISE DRESSING

Egg yolk, 1.
Cooking or olive oil.
Lemon juice.
Salt.
Sugar, 1 tablespoonful.

Into a saucer break the yolk of a fresh egg; add to it a large pinch of salt, and with a fork stir the yolk till it begins to stiffen. Gradually add to the yolk, a drop at a time, cooking oil or olive oil, stirring well after each drop is added. Continue this process till the mixture becomes too stiff to stir, then thin it with lemon juice, and add more salt. The salt helps to stiffen it. Thicken again with oil in the same manner as before, and thin again with lemon juice. Continue this till the desired amount is made. When stiff enough to cut with a knife, add one tablespoonful of sugar.

This will keep for a number of days, if set on ice. Success in making this depends upon the care with which the oil is added; at first, a drop at a time, and towards the last adding two or three drops, and perhaps half a teaspoonful at a time.

Note.—To make it keep well, add one tablespoonful boiling water, beaten in quickly. To keep from curdling, put lemon juice and oil on ice for fifteen minutes before using.

(31)

WHITE DRESSING

Egg yolk, 1, light colored.
Salt.
Cracked ice.
Cream, whipped to stiff froth, 6 tablepoonfuls.
Oil, 6 tablespoonfuls.
Lemon juice, 1 tablespoonful.

Drop the yolk into a cold bowl, mix lightly, add
a small pinch of salt; then add the oil drop by drop.
The dressing should be very thick. Stand the bowl
in another containing a little cracked ice, so that
you may be constantly reducing the color of the egg.
Now add slowly the lemon juice, then stir in the
whipped cream. This dressing, if properly made,
should be almost as white as whipped cream, while
having the flavor of mayonnaise. Serve with Waldorf salad.

BOILED SALAD DRESSING

Eggs, 5.
Melted butter, ¼ cup.
Lemon juice, 4 tablespoonfuls.
Salt, 1 level teaspoonful.
Sugar, 1 level teaspoonful.
Rich cream, 1 cup.

To the yolks add the salt and sugar; beat with an
egg whisk until thick and light, then add gradually
the melted butter and lemon juice. Cook over hot
water until the mixture thickens and falls away from
the sides of the pan. Take from stove, put into a
glass jar, and when cool cover closely. When ready

to use pour into it lightly the rich cream whipped to a stiff, dry froth. If whipped cream can not conveniently be obtained, plain sweet or sour cream may be used in the dressing, but it will not be so light and flaky.

CREAM SALAD DRESSING (PLAIN)

Lemon juice, ½ cup.
Sugar, 1 tablespoonful.
Rich milk or cream, ½ cup.
Olive oil, 1 tablespoonful.
Salt, 1 teaspoonful.
Eggs well beaten, 2.

Put the lemon juice into a granite dish on the stove, and add the olive oil, sugar, and salt. Put the milk or cream on the stove in another saucepan, and when hot add the beaten eggs. Let cook smooth, but do not allow it to boil or it will curdle. Remove from the stove, and when partially cool beat the two sauces together. This is a very nice dressing for vegetable salads.

CREAM SALAD DRESSING

Cream, 1 cup.
Milk, cold.
Butter, size of walnut.
Salt, 1 level teaspoonful.
Lemon juice, 4 tablespoonfuls.
Corn starch, 1 rounded teaspoonful.
Eggs, 2.
Sugar, 1 level teaspoonful.

Put the cream into a double boiler; when scalding

3

hot add the corn starch dissolved in a little cold milk, and cook about five minutes, stirring constantly. Then add the butter. To the yolks of the eggs add the salt and sugar; beat till light and thick, then add alternately the lemon juice and the hot cooked mixture. Fold in the stiffly beaten whites, and set aside to become cold.

This dressing may be used the same as mayonnaise.

WHITE CREAM SALAD DRESSING

Make same as cream salad dressing, omitting the yolks of the eggs.

FRENCH SALAD DRESSING

Oil, 3 tablespoonfuls.
Salt.
Lemon juice, 1 tablespoonful.
Onion juice, ¼ teaspoonful.

Mix and pour over the salad.

LETTUCE DRESSING

Hard-boiled eggs, 3.
Lemon juice, ½ cup.
Lettuce.
Olive oil, 1 tablespoonful.
Salt.

Mash the yolks smooth and fine, add the olive oil and salt. Mix well, and add gradually the lemon juice. Beat thoroughly, then pour the dressing over the lettuce. Cut the whites of the eggs into rings and lay on top. Serve as soon as dressed.

GOLDEN SALAD DRESSING

Pineapple juice, ¼ cup.
Lemon juice, ¼ cup.
Beaten eggs, 2.
Sugar, ⅓ cup.

After beating the eggs well, add the pineapple juice, lemon juice, sugar, and small pinch of salt. Beat together and cook in double boiler. Let boil about two minutes.

NUT OR OLIVE OIL SALAD DRESSING

Olive oil, ½ cup.
Water, ¼ cup.
Lemon juice, ¼ cup.
Salt, 1 teaspoonful.
Beaten eggs, 3.

Beat all well together in the dish; set dish in hot water over the fire, and stir constantly till thickened. As soon as it begins to thicken remove from the fire and place in a dish of cold water, stirring until it cools, and set on ice till cold. It is then ready for use.

OIL SALAD DRESSING (SOUR)

Lemon juice, 2 teaspoonfuls.
Olive oil, ¼ cup.
Salt, ½ teaspoonful.
Water, 2 teaspoonfuls.
Eggs, 2.

Heat together in double boiler, stirring constantly. When it begins to thicken, place into cold water and stir until cold.

GREEN MAYONNAISE

Make as ordinary mayonnaise. Use two light-colored yolks and six tablespoonfuls of oil. Chop enough parsley to make one tablespoonful; put it into a bowl, and with a knife rub it to a pulp. Then add gradually to the mayonnaise. Add a teaspoonful of the lemon juice. Use for fruit salad, white grapes, and pulp of shaddock. Mix, and serve on lettuce leaves.

DRESSING LA BLANCHE

Butter, 1½ dessertspoonfuls.
Flour, 1 heaped dessertspoonful.
Salt.
Egg, 1.
Lemon juice, ¼ cup.

Melt the butter in a frying-pan, but be careful not to brown it. When hot, stir in the flour, well-beaten yolk, lemon juice, and salt to taste. Stir this dressing through the vegetables, and serve on a garnish of crisp lettuce.

SOUPS

SOUPS

Cream soups are seasonable at any time, using any vegetable in its season. Canned goods may be used when the fresh article is not obtainable.

Vegetables that are too tough and old to cook in any other way may be used in soups to advantage. If it can be afforded, a teaspoonful of whipped cream may be dropped into each plate, and will be found very delicious.

By a puree is meant a thick soup; it differs but little from cream soup, being perhaps a trifle thicker. If properly made, cream soups and purees are dainty, delicious, and nourishing.

Fruit soups are in favor during hot weather, for dinners and luncheons; they are very easily made, and are wholesome and refreshing. Any desired fruit juice may be thickened with corn starch, sago, or arrowroot, and served with or without fruit.

Fruit soup should always be served cold, in glass sherbet cups, with a layer of chipped ice on top.

KINDS OF SOUP

Observing these proportions and following the foregoing directions, delicious cream soups are made of rice, squash, celery, peas, asparagus, cucumber, spinach, peanuts, potato, corn, lima beans, cauliflower, beets, tomato, salsify, chestnut, mushrooms, onions, baked beans, lentils, macaroni, spaghetti, watercress, string beans, sago, tapioca, barley, carrots, etc. All vegetables should be cooked very tender in boiling salted water, drained, and rubbed through a sieve. Rice, sago, tapioca, and barley should be boiled slowly till each grain is soft and distinct. Roasted peanuts are chopped fine; chestnuts are boiled and mashed; macaroni and spaghetti are cut into very small pieces, after boiling till tender. String beans are to be minced before adding to the soup.

CREAM SOUPS, FOUNDATION OF

Rub one heaping tablespoonful of butter and two of sifted flour to a cream; melt in a saucepan over the fire, and add slowly four cups milk, stirring constantly. When it thickens add salt and whatever seasoning and ingredient is desired to make the soup.

CROUTONS FOR SOUP

Take thin slices of bread, cut them into little squares, place them in a baking pan, and brown to a golden color in a quick oven.

EGG BALLS FOR SOUP

Egg yolks, hard boiled, 6.
Salt, 1 teaspoonful.
Flour, ½ tablespoonful.
Egg yolks, raw, 2.

Rub the hard-boiled yolks and flour smooth, then add the raw yolks and the salt. Mix all well together, make into balls, and drop into the soup a few minutes before serving.

EGG DUMPLINGS FOR SOUP

Milk, 1 cup.
Flour.
Eggs, 2.

Beat the eggs well, add the milk and as much flour as will make a smooth, rather thick batter, free from lumps. Drop this batter, a tablespoonful at a time, into the boiling soup.

NOODLES FOR SOUP

Beat one egg till light, add a pinch of salt and flour enough to make a stiff dough. Roll out very thin; sprinkle with flour to keep from sticking. Then roll up into a scroll, begin at the end, and slice into strips as thin as straws. After all are cut, mix them lightly together, and to prevent their sticking together keep them floured a little till you are ready to drop them into the soup, which should be done a few minutes before serving. If boiled too long they go to pieces.

VEGETABLE BOUILLON

Vegetable soup stock, 2 quarts.
Cooked and strained tomatoes, 2 cups.
Bay leaves, 2.
Salt, 1 tablespoonful.
Onions, grated, medium size, 2.

Mix all the ingredients together, and let simmer

slowly two or three hours. There should be about one quart of soup when done; strain, reheat, and serve.

NUT CHOWDER SOUP

Nuttolene or protose, ¼ pound.
Hard-boiled eggs, 3.
Browned onions, 3.
Sage, 1 teaspoonful.
Thyme, 1 teaspoonful.
Bay leaves, 2.
Salt, 1 tablespoonful.

Chop all together till fine, then add to strained boiling tomatoes, four cups; add boiling water, one cup; thicken with flour, one tablespoonful; reheat and serve.

NUT FRENCH SOUP

Vegetable soup stock, 1½ quarts.
Tomatoes, cooked, strained, 2 cups.
Sage, ¼ teaspoonful.
Browned flour, 1 tablespoonful rounded.
Onions, large, 1.
Bay leaves, 2.
Thyme, ½ teaspoonful.
Salt to taste.

Slice the onion and mix all the ingredients together, excepting the salt; boil slowly one hour; strain, reheat, salt, and serve. This soup requires plenty of salt to bring out the flavor.

MOCK CHICKEN SOUP

Butter, ¼ cup.
Onion, medium size, 1.
Celery stalks, 1.
Milk, 1¼ quarts.
One egg.
Flour, 2 tablespoonfuls.
Parsley, chopped fine, 1 teaspoonful.
Nuttolene, 3 tablespoonfuls.
Flour.

Put butter in saucepan with the onion, parsley, and celery; cook it to a golden brown color; add the flour and cook until brown, being careful not to scorch. Now add the milk boiling hot and stir briskly to prevent lumping. Add the nuttolene. Beat the egg with enough flour to make a stiff batter, but thin enough to pour; pour this into the boiling stock, stirring at the same time. This will appear as small dumplings in the soup. Let simmer twenty or thirty minutes; salt, and serve.

MOCK CHICKEN BROTH

Small white beans, 2 cups.
Small onion, 1.
Salt.
Hot water, 8 cups.
Celery salt.
Butter.

Wash, then stew the beans in hot water with the onion for three hours, stewing down to six cups; strain, and add a pinch of celery salt and a small

piece of butter. Salt to taste. This broth may be
served to the sick instead of beef tea.

PLAIN VEGETABLE SOUP (1)

For soup stock.

> Water, 6 cups.
> Strained tomatoes, 2 cups.

Shave in fine shreds, add to soup stock, and cook
moderately for two hours.

> Carrot, 1.
> Potato, 1.
> Leek. 1.
> Turnip, 1.
> Onions, 2.
> Celery stalk, 1.

Add a little sage and thyme. When done, run
through puree sieve or colander, and add a little
chopped parsley and salt to taste.

PLAIN VEGETABLE SOUP (2)

> Butter, 2 tablespoonfuls.
> Flour, 1 tablespoonful.
> Chopped onion, 1.
> Chopped carrots, ½ cup.
> Chopped potatoes, ½ cup.
> Chopped turnips, ½ cup.
> Chopped celery, ½ cup.

Place in heated saucepan, stir often to prevent
burning, add a little more butter if necessary; brown
till vegetables are quite soft, then add

> Strained tomatoes, 2 cups.
> Hot water to proper consistency.

Season with parsley and salt to taste. Simmer till done.

WHITE SOUBISE SOUP

Bread, 4 or 5 slices.
Onions, 4.
Salt, 1 teaspoonful.
Butter, 1 teaspoonful.
Rich milk, 2 cups.
Potatoes, 2.
Flour, 1 teaspoonful.
Water, 4 cups.

Soak the bread in the milk, boil onions and potatoes in water until well done, and mix with the bread and milk; add salt and flour rubbed in the butter; strain all through a fine sieve; bring again to the boiling point, but do not allow it to boil; serve. If too thick, add a little boiling water.

JULIENNE SOUP

Fresh peas, ⅓ cup.
Chopped potatoes, ¾ cup.
Tomato, ¼ cup.
Soup stock, 1 quart.
Carrots cut in dice, ½ cup.
Chopped turnips, ⅓ cup.
Minced onion, 1.
Chopped parsley.

Cook the turnips and carrots together in just enough water to prevent scorching, the potatoes and onions in the same manner, the peas by themselves. When all are done, mix together and add the soup stock, salt, and parsley; reheat, and serve. The water the vegetables are cooked in should be used in the soup.

TOMATO SOUP

Soup stock, 3 cups.
Nut butter, 1 tablespoonful.
Strained tomatoes, 2 cups.
Salt.

Add tomatoes to soup stock, also the nut butter mixed smooth and thin in a little of the tomato; heat to boiling, salt, and serve.

BEAN AND TOMATO SOUP

Boiled beans, 1 cup.
Butter, 1 tablespoonful.
Cooked rice, ¼ cup.
Salt.
Stewed tomatoes, 1 cup.
Flour, 1 tablespoonful.
Boiling water to required consistency.

Rub beans and tomatoes through a sieve; add salt and butter rubbed in flour; then add cooked rice and enough boiling water to make the proper consistency; reheat, and serve.

TOMATO-VERMICELLI SOUP

Strained tomatoes, 3 cups.
Vermicelli, ½ cup.
Water, 2 cups.

Cook the vermicelli in the tomato till done and add water; if too thin, bind with a little thickening of butter and flour. A rounded tablespoonful of each will be enough for each quart of soup.

TOMATO AND OKRA SOUP

Onion, large, 1.
Butter.
Stewed tomatoes, 2 cups.
Soup stock or water, 4 cups.
Thinly sliced okra pods, 2 cups.
Flour, 1 teaspoonful.
Nut butter, 1 teaspoonful.
Chopped parsley.
Salt.

Brown onion in a saucepan with a little butter; add flour, nut butter, tomatoes, parsley, and okra. Add the soup stock or water and cook slowly for three hours. Season with salt, and serve.

WHITE SWISS SOUP

Rice, ½ cup.
Onion, small, 1.
Rich milk, 1½ cups.
Flour, ½ teaspoonful.
Water, 2 cups.
Potato, 1.
Egg yolk, 1.
Salt.

Boil the rice in the water, and add the onion and potato. When the vegetables are well done add the rich milk and bring to a boil. Beat well the yolk of the egg with the flour and stir in the boiling soup. Let it boil, season with salt, rub through a sieve; reheat. and serve.

CORN AND TOMATO SOUP

Kornlet, ground fine, 1½ cups.
Strained tomatoes, 2 cups.
Water, 1 cup.

Mix thoroughly, season with salt, heat to a boiling point, and serve.

CEREAL CONSOMME

Cooking oil, ¼ cup.
Chopped onion, 1.
Flour, 1 tablespoonful.
Crushed protose, ½ pound.
Caramel-cereal, 1 cup.
Salt.
Barley, ¼ cup.
Carrot, small,1, finely chopped.
Boiling water, 6 cups.
Bay leaf.

Place in the soup kettle the cooking oil and barley; brown barley till quite brown; add onion, carrot, flour, and brown the vegetables till quite tender; add the protose and boiling water; let simmer very gently for six hours, adding boiling water from time to time. Keep the original amount. Stir often to prevent burning. Half an hour before the soup is done add the caramel-cereal, bay leaf, and salt; press through a fine colander, and simmer to six cups.

SWISS LENTIL SOUP

Lentils, 1 cup.
Small onion, 1.
Browned flour, 2 rounded tablespoonfuls.
Salt.

Put lentils to cook in a large quantity of boiling water; boil rapidly a short time, then simmer without stirring. When they begin to get tender and are yet quite moist, slice an onion and press into the lentils until covered; keep the vessel over a slow, even fire, until the lentils are well dried out. The drying-out may be finished in the oven if the lentils are covered so that they will not harden on top. When well dried add a little boiling water and rub through a fine colander, removing the hulls. Into this pulp stir the browned flour. Beat till smooth, then add gradually enough boiling water to make of consistency of soup; salt, boil, and set where it will keep hot twenty minutes to an hour, to blend ingredients.

SPRING VEGETABLE SOUP

> Green peas, 1 cup.
> Onion, 1.
> Egg yolk, 1.
> Soup stock, 3 cups.
> Salt.
> Shredded lettuce, 1 head.
> Parsley, 1 small bunch.
> Water, 1 cup.
> Butter, size of egg.

Put in the stew-pan the lettuce, onion, parsley, and butter, with the water; let simmer till tender; season with salt; when done strain off the vegetables and put two-thirds of the liquid in the stock. Beat up the yolk with the other third. Put it over the fire,

4

and at the moment of serving add this with the vegetables to the soup.

TURNIP AND RICE SOUP

> Turnip, medium sized, 1.
> Milk, 3 cups.
> Butter.
> Washed rice, ⅓ cup.
> Cream, 1 cup.
> Croutons or toast.

Pare a medium-sized turnip, slice, and put with rice and butter into saucepan with sufficient water to cook; let simmer till tender, rub through a fine sieve and return to the saucepan. Mix in enough milk to make of the proper consistency; stir over the fire and let simmer ten or fifteen minutes; then stir in a lump of butter and cream; serve with croutons.

GERMAN LENTIL SOUP

> Lentils, ¾ cup.
> Carrot, a few slices.
> Nut butter, 1 tablespoonful.
> Celery, one sprig, or a little celery salt.
> Salt.
> Water, 4 cups.
> Turnips, a few slices.
> Apple sauce, ½ cup.
> Onion, 1.

Boil lentils in the water with the onion, carrot, turnip, and celery; boil gently about one and one-half hours; put through a sieve and return to soup kettle;

add nut butter and apple sauce. Bring to a boil,
salt, and serve.

If necessary, add a little boiling water or rich
milk to thin the soup.

LENTIL AND TOMATO SOUP

Lentils, 1 cup.
Water, 4 cups.
Nut butter, 1 tablespoonful.
Salt.
Onion, 1.
Stewed tomatoes, 2 cups.
Browned flour, 1 tablespoonful.

Stew the lentils with the onion in the water one
hour; add stewed tomatoes, nut butter, and browned
flour; bring to a brisk boil, season with salt, press
through a colander, reheat, and serve.

RICE AND NUT SOUP

Vegetable stock, 5 cups.
Sage, ¼ teaspoonful.
Rice, 3 tablespoonfuls.
Salt.

Boil twenty minutes and serve.

BARLEY AND NUT SOUP

Rice, 2 tablespoonfuls.
Vegetable stock, 4 cups.
Barley, ¼ cup.
Salt.

Cook the barley and rice until perfectly done in

about one and one-half cups of water; add stock, salt to taste, reheat, and serve.

NUT AND OLIVE SOUP

Soup stock, 4 cups.
Ripe olives, chopped, 12.
Browned flour, 1 tablespoonful.
Tomato, strained, ½ cup.
Lemon juice, 1 teaspoonful.
Nut butter, 2 tablespoonfuls.

Emulsify the nut butter in a little of the stock, add the remaining stock and the rest of the ingredients, except the browned flour, which should be added after the soup has boiled.   Salt, and serve.

LENTIL AND NUT SOUP

Lentils, ¾ cup.
Oil, 1 tablespoonful.
Large onion, 1.
Vegetable stock, 4 cups.

Cook lentils till tender and put through a colander; in the meantime brown the chopped onion in the oil; add to the lentil pulp, mix with stock, salt, reheat, and serve.

NUT NOODLE SOUP

Vegetable soup stock, 6 cups.
Nut butter, 2 tablespoonfuls.
Noodles.

Mix the nut butter in a little of the stock until smooth and thin; then add remainder of stock, salt, boil, add noodles, cook about twenty minutes, serve.

NUT AND PEA SOUP

Green peas, 4 cups.
Vegetable soup stock, 6 cups.
Salt, 2 tablespoonfuls.

Boil peas till tender, rub through a colander, and add to soup stock. Salt, reheat, and serve.

NUT AND BEAN SOUP

Beans, 1 cup.
Salt, 1 tablespoonful.
Vegetable soup stock, 4 cups.
A little thyme.

Cook beans in just enough water to prevent scorching. When done rub through a sieve or colander; add the vegetable soup stock, thyme, and salt. Reheat, and serve.

NUT AND ASPARAGUS SOUP

Finely cut asparagus, 4 cups.
Vegetable soup stock, 4 cups.
Salt.

Cook till asparagus is very tender; put through a sieve; add stock and salt; reheat, and serve.

BROWN BEAN SOUP

Water, 2 quarts.
Tomatoes, 1 cup.
Onion, ¼.
Small bunch of herbs, anise, laurel, etc.
Salt.
Brown beans, 1 cup.
Leek, ¼.
Juice of 1 lemon.

Cook beans in water till soft, then add vegetables and herbs; after the soup is boiled, add the lemon juice; rub through a sieve; salt, reheat, and serve.

WHITE BEAN SOUP

White beans, 1 cup.
Onion, medium sized, 1.
Salt, 1 teaspoonful.
Water, 2 quarts.
Nut butter, 1 tablespoonful.

Stew the beans and onions in the water until tender; add nut butter and salt; press through a sieve, bring to a boil, and serve. The addition of some cream will improve this soup.

SAGO SOUP

Sago, ½ cup.
Egg, 1.
Boiling milk, 4 cups.
Boiled cream.

Wash the sago, add it to the boiling milk, and simmer till the sago is dissolved and forms a sort of jelly. At the moment of serving add the beaten yolk of an egg and a little cream previously boiled.

BEAN TAPIOCA

White beans, ¾ cup.
Tapioca, ½ cup.
Salt.
Water, 4 cups.
Hot water.
Cream.

Cook beans in water till well done; press through a strainer, add tapioca, and cook till clear; add hot water to make of proper consistency; season with salt and cream; heat well, and serve.

GREEN PEA SOUP

>Green peas, in pod, 4 quarts.
>Spinach leaves, 1 handful.
>Sliced lettuce, 1 head.
>Dash of lemon juice.
>Salt, ½ teaspoonful.
>Sugar, 1 teaspoonful.
>Boiling water, 6 cups.
>Cucumber sliced, ½.

Shell peas and throw into a dish of cold water; break the shells and put them into a kettle with boiling water; set over the fire and simmer half and hour. Remove pods, and add lettuce, spinach, salt and sugar. Let boil till the spinach and lettuce are pulpy, take up, and run through a puree sieve; boil the peas and cucumber in a little water, mash and rub through a sieve; mix with the soup, season with salt and a dash of lemon juice. Serve with croutons.

RICE SOUP

>Rice, ¼ cup.
>Salt, 1 teaspoonful.
>Milk, 3 cups.
>Butter, 1 tablespoonful.
>Water, 3 cups.
>Egg yolk, 1.
>Flour, 2 teaspoonfuls.

Boil the rice in the water for forty minutes, or until prefectly soft, adding salt; add sufficient boiling water from time to time to keep the original amount; press through a sieve and thicken with well-beaten yolk of egg, milk, flour, and butter. Add a little more salt if necessary; serve with toasted crackers or zwieback sprinkled with crumbs of cottage cheese.

LIMA BEAN SOUP

Lima bean soup may be prepared same as white bean soup, omitting the tapioca.

BREAD BISQUE

Dry sifted bread crumbs, one cup, added to cream soup, four cups.

TOMATO BISQUE NO. 1

Tomatoes, ½ quart can.
Flour, 1 tablespoonful.
Nut butter, 1 tablespoonful.
Milk, 4 cups.
Butter, 1 tablespoonful.
Salt.
Bay leaf, 1.
Onion, small, 1.

Place butter in pot, add one bay leaf, one small onion; let braize till light brown, add flour, and stir until flour is well mixed; add hot milk, slowly stir-ring constantly to keep smooth; add nut butter, which should be emulsified first with the tomato, then add slowly stirring briskly; salt, heat thor-oughly, strain; reheat, serve.

TOMATO BISQUE NO. 2

Strained tomatoes, 4 cups.
Peanut butter, about 4 tablespoonfuls.
Salt.

Put tomatoes in double boiler, set on the range, and when scalding hot add the nut butter emulsified in enough water to pour readily, mix together and salt to taste. Use plenty of salt to bring out the flavor.

ROLLED OATS SOUP

Chopped onion, 1.
Celery salt.
Left-over porridge, 1 cup.
Milk, 2 cups.
Butter, 1 tablespoonful.
Bay leaf.
Water, 2 cups.
Salt, 1 teaspoonful.

Into a saucepan put the chopped onion and butter; cook carefully, without browning the butter, until the onion is perfectly soft; then add celery salt, bay leaf, and porridge; stir for a moment, then add water and milk; bring to a boil and strain; add salt, reheat, and serve.

FAMILY FAVORITE

Soup stock, 4 cups.
Sliced okra, 1 pod.
Salt.
Stewed tomatoes, ½ cup.
Water, 1 cup.

Mix all together and boil one hour; strain, reheat, and serve.

NUT MEAT BROTH

Water, 4 cups.
Almond meal, 1 cup.
Gluten meal or browned flour, 2 tablespoonfuls.
Salt.

Let all boil together thoroughly, and serve.

PEA SOUP WITH VEGETABLE STOCK

Scotch peas, 1 cup.
Vegetable soup stock, 4 cups.
Mint, ¼ teaspoonful.
Salt.

Cook peas till soft and put through a fine colander to remove the hulls. Add soup stock and mint, reheat, salt, and serve.

A cup of cream is a great improvement to this soup.

SAVORY POTATO SOUP

Vegetable soup stock, 4 cups.
Potatoes, medium size, 2 or 3.
Mint, ⅓ teaspoonful.
Chopped onion, 1.
Salt, 1 teaspoonful.
Marjoram, ¼ teaspoonful.

Cook the potatoes and onion till soft. Put through a colander, add the soup stock, mint, marjoram, and salt, which have been simmered together half an hour. Heat well, and serve.

CELERY AND TOMATO SOUP

Celery heart, 1.
Soup stock, 2 cups.
Celery salt.
Tomato, 2 cups.
Salt.

Chop celery rather fine, and cook in a little water till tender; add the tomato, salt, and soup stock; heat well, and serve.

NUT AND CREAM OF CORN SOUP

Sweet corn rubbed fine, 1 quart can.
Vegetable soup stock, 4 cups.
Salt, 1 heaping tablespoonful.

Bring to a boil, rub through a colander, reheat, and serve.

ARTICHOKE SOUP

Artichokes, 6.
Onions, small, 2.
Sage, ¼ teaspoonful.
Lemon juice, 1 tablespoonful.
Salt.
Water, 2 quarts.
Protose, ⅛ pound.
Bay leaf.
Browned flour, 1 tablespoonful.

Select prime, green, globe artichokes before they have developed; cut off the stems, trim off the hard leaves round the bottom, and cut off the upper quarter of the artichoke leaves. Put the water in soup kettle; add the artichoke, onions, and protose. Let simmer gently for two hours, then add sage, bay leaf, and lemon juice. Thicken with browned flour. Let all boil together a few minutes, then press through a colander, salt, reheat, and serve.

IMPROMPTU SOUP NO. 1

Onion, 1.

Slice into heated saucepan with

Savory or green herbs, 1 pinch.
Butter, 1 tablespoonful.

Let brown two or three minutes, then add

Nut butter, 1 tablespoonful.

Brown a little longer, then add

Stewed tomatoes, 1 cup.
Hot water, 3 cups.

Let all boil together and thicken with gluten; salt, strain, and serve.

IMPROMPTU SOUP NO. 2

Malted nuts, ½ cup.
Browned flour, 1 tablespoonful.
Flour, 1 tablespoonful.

Mix, and dissolve in a little milk, then add

Milk, 3 cups

and heat to boiling point, stirring often to prevent scorching; set back far enough to keep from boiling, then whip into the broth

Eggs well beaten, 4.

Salt. and serve.

CREOLE SOUP

Water, 2 cups.
Tomatoes, 1 pint.
Clove of garlic, 1.
Small turnip, 1.
Boiled rice, heaped tablespoonful.
Small carrot, 1.

Boil all together, season with a little salt, rub the vegetables through a sieve, and thin to the consistency of cream with hot water or nut cream.

PALESTINE SOUP

Jerusalem artichokes, 12.
Celery, 1 sprig.
Boiled cream, 1 pint.
Croutons.
Leek, 1 sprig.
Salt.
Nutmeg.

Wash and peel the artichokes, put over them cold water sufficient to cover, add leeks, celery, and salt. Simmer an hour and a half. Press through a sieve, put back on the stove, and beat into it a pint of boiled cream. Add a little nutmeg. Serve with croutons. If too thick, add a little hot milk or cream.

FRUIT SOUP (PINEAPPLE)

Thicken pineapple juice with arrowroot. Serve cold with a bit of pineapple glace in each cup.

62

CHOCOLATE SOUP

Chocolate (Sanitas), ¼ pound.
Water, 2½ cups.
Sugar, 2 tablespoonfuls.
Flour, 1 tablespoonful.
Milk, 1 quart.
Ground cinnamon, 1 teaspoonful.
Whipped cream, 1 cup.

Soak the chocolate in two cups of the water; when soft put to cook; when it boils add the sugar and flour rubbed smooth in the rest of the water. Cook slowly for five minutes and add the hot milk. Strain, stir in the cinnamon and whipped cream. Serve at once with crisps or wafers. Blanched almonds toasted are served with the soup.

FRUIT SOUP

Strawberry, or other juice, 1 cup.
Pineapple juice, 1 cup.
Lemon juice, 1 tablespoonful.
Sago, 1 tablespoonful.
Sugar, 1 tablespoonful.
Chopped ice.

With the strawberry or other juice cook the sago; add the pineapple juice and sugar; cool, and serve in sherbet cups with chipped ice.

FRUIT SOUP (SWEDISH)

Boil prunes and raisins slowly till tender, sweeten and save the juice; boil sago till clear, mix with the fruit and juice, and serve very cold.

FRUIT SOUP (ORANGE)

Thicken orange juice with arrowroot, and serve very cold in cups with a bit of candied orange peel on top of each glass.

FRUIT SOUP (LEMON)

Make a strong lemonade, thicken with arrowroot, serve very cold with a bit of candied lemon peel or candied ginger in each glass.

FRUIT SOUP (MARQUISE)

Take two parts red raspberry juice and one of currant, sweeten, thicken with arrowroot and sago; candied orange peel or blanched and shredded almonds are a dainty addition.

FRUIT SOUP (CRANBERRY)

Thicken some sweetened cranberry juice with arrowroot, and serve cold in cups, as a first course at a Christmas or New Year's dinner.

FRUIT SOUP (GRAPE)

Thicken bottled grape juice with arrowroot, and serve cold with chipped ice. This is refreshing for invalids.

FRUIT SOUP (CHERRY)

Thicken cherry juice with arrowroot, and serve with other fruit soups; garnish with black cherries in their season.

FRUIT SOUP (STRAWBERRY)

Thicken fresh strawberry juice with arrowroot and put on ice to chill; put a layer of chipped ice on top of each cup before serving, and lay a ripe strawberry, stem and all, on top of each glass.

RAISIN, APPLE, OR PRUNE SOUP

Either seedless raisins, apples, or prunes may be added to sago soup. The soup should then bear the name of the fruit used.

ENTREES

MOCK WHITE FISH

Rice flour, 1/3 cup.
Butter, 1 scant teaspoonful.
Mace, 1/4 teaspoonful.
Salt to taste.
Milk, 1 cup.
Onion grated, 1 tablespoonful.
Potatoes, mashed, 3 cups.

Heat the milk to boiling, stir in the rice, flour, butter, onion, mace, and salt. Cook all ten minutes, stirring frequently. Have the potatoes ready, freshly cooked and mashed; while hot add the rice mixture, and put into a pan to cool. When cool, cut in slices about five inches long, dip in egg and crumbs, put in oiled pan, and bake until nicely browned. Serve with parsley sauce.

FILLETS OF VEGETARIAN SALMON

Milk, 1 1/2 cups.
Farina, 1/2 cup.
Tomatoes, cooked and strained, 1/2 cup.
Egg, 1.
Salt to taste
Nuttolene, 1/2 cup.
Eggplant, boiled and mashed, 1 1/2 cups.
Bread crumbs, fine and dry, 1 cup.
Color, vegetable red enough to make salmon color.

Cook and mash the eggplant, stir the nuttolene to a cream in a little of the milk, then add the rest of

(67)

the milk, the eggplant, tomatoes, and salt. Set in double boiler; when scalding hot, add the farina and bread crumbs. Mix thoroughly and let cook fifteen or twenty minutes. Remove from the range, stir in the raw egg and the color, mixing till the color is perfectly blended. Turn into a deep pan to cool; should be about two inches deep. When cold cut into slices, egg, crumb, and bake. Serve with parsley sauce.

PROTOSE ROAST WITH OLIVE SAUCE

> Protose, ¾ pound.
> Chopped onion, small, 1.
> Parsley, 1 tablespoonful.
> Boiling water, 2 cups.
> Butter, 1 tablespoonful.
> Bread crumbs, 2 cups.
> Eggs, 2.
> Salt to taste.

Put the onion, parsley, and butter into the boiling water, and thicken with bread crumbs stiff enough to cut nicely when done. Into this mixture put one hard-boiled egg chopped fine, and break in one raw egg to make it hold together. Salt to taste. Put a layer of this filling into a baking-pan, then a layer of protose cut in thin slices, then a layer of the filling, and another layer of the protose, and last another layer of the filling. Bake in a moderate oven one hour. Serve with olive sauce.

MOCK TURKEY WITH DRESSING

German lentils, 1 cup.
Chopped walnut meats, ½ cup.
Milk, 1 cup.
Salt.
Celery salt.
Granola or bread crumbs.
Minced onion, ¼ cup.
Chopped celery, 1 cup.
Eggs, 2.
Sage.
Sliced bread.

1. Thoroughly wash the lentils and soak overnight. Boil slowly until tender and run through colander. Add the walnut meats, one egg, and the minced onion browned with the chopped celery in a little oil. Add salt and sage to taste. Thicken with granola or bread crumbs.

2. Dip thin slices of bread in a mixture of one egg and a cup of milk, or thin slices of nuttolene may be used instead.

Make alternate layers of 1 and 2.

DRESSING NO. 1

Stale bread crumbs.
Hot milk, 2 cups.
Eggs, 1 or 2.
Butter, 1 tablespoonful.

Mix bread crumbs with hot milk, eggs, and butter. Season with salt, sage, and onions. Serve with cranberry sauce.

DRESSING NO. 2

Large onions, 2.
Fresh bread crumbs, 1 cup.
Milk, ¾ cup.
Sage, 1 tablespoonful.
Beaten eggs, 2.
Chopped parsley, 2 tablespoonfuls.
Butter, ¼ cup.
Salt to taste.

Peel onions and parboil. Drain and chop fine. Soak bread crumbs in the milk; then mix all ingredients together. Stir the mixture over the fire until it is reduced to a thick paste, without allowing it to boil.

Serve a slice of the roast with a spoonful of dressing on one end and cranberry sauce on the other.

ROAST DUCK (VEGETARIAN STYLE)

Lentil pulp, 1¾ cups.
Minced onion, ¼ cup.
Chopped parsley, ⅓ cup.
Stale bread crumbs, ground fine, 1 cup.
Eggs (one hard-boiled), 3.
Butter, 1 teaspoonful.
Chopped walnuts, ½ cup.

Take lentil pulp, one hard-boiled egg chopped fine, one beaten egg, minced onion, and chopped parsley browned in a little oil, one teaspoonful of butter, and salt to taste. Mix well and put one-half of this mixture in an oiled baking pan, then a layer of the following mixture: Stale bread crumbs soaked in hot water, chopped walnuts, a little grated

onion, one egg, and salt and sage to taste. Finish
with a layer of the lentil mixture. Bake, and serve
with gravy.

NUTTOLENE ROAST

Nuttolene, 1 pound.
Bread crumbs.
Hot water, 1 quart.
Salt and sage to taste.

Put the nuttolene through a vegetable press, or
work smooth with a knife or spoon; add the hot
water and beat to a cream. Add salt and sage, and
thicken with bread crumbs stiff enough to retain its
shape when moulded. Press into a deep buttered
bread-pan and bake till nicely browned. Turn out
of the pan and slice. Serve with any good brown
sauce or walnut gravy.

MOCK VEAL LOAF

Nuttolene, ¼ pound.
Minced protose, ½ pound.
Egg, well beaten, 1.
Milk, ¼ cup.
Sage, ¼ teaspoonful.
Ground mace, ¼ teaspoonful.
Butter size of an egg.
1 small onion, braized in the butter.

Cracker or zwieback crumbs enough to make a
stiff mixture. Mix all together, salt to taste, and
bake in a deep bread-pan. Garnish with parsley or
young celery hearts.

VEGETARIAN ROAST

Nut food, ⅓ pound.
Onion, ½.
Egg, 1.
Hot water, 2 cups.
Butter, 2 teaspoonfuls.
Bread crumbs or granola.

To the water add the nut food minced, minced and browned onion, and butter. Thicken with toasted bread crumbs or granola until quite stiff. Add the beaten egg, salt, and a little sage if desired. Put in oiled pan and bake. Serve with gravy.

ROAST OF PROTOSE

Protose, 1 pound.
Strained tomato, ½ cup.
Chopped onion, 1.
Nut butter, 2 tablespoonfuls.
Browned flour, 2 tablespoonfuls.
Sage.

Cut the protose lengthwise through the center, then cut each half in six pieces. Place in a deep baking-pan, let the first piece lean slantingly against the end or side of the pan, the second against the first, and so on. Sprinkle this with finely chopped onion, and a little powdered sage, and pour over it a nut cream made of two heaping tablespoonfuls of nut butter emulsified, in enough hot water to cover the protose. Add to this the browned flour, rubbed smooth in a little tomato. Salt to taste. A little celery salt may be used if desired. Cover and bake till the gravy is thick and brown.

HAMBURGER LOAF

Lentils, raw, 1 cup.
Protose, ½ pound.
Cooking oil, 2 tablespoonfuls.
Salt.
Chopped onion, ½ cup.
Eggs, 5.
Bread crumbs.

Cook the lentils until tender, then simmer as dry as possible. Put through a colander, brown the onions in oil, and add to the lentils, together with the protose and two of the raw eggs. Mix salt to taste, and add enough bread crumbs so that it will mold nicely.

Have the three remaining eggs boiled hard and the shells removed. Put one-half the loaf mixture into a bread-pan, then put the three hard-boiled eggs in a row through the center and cover with the remaining mixture. Press down gently and bake. Serve with sauce imperial.

NUT AND GRANOLA ROAST

Minced nut food, ¼ pound.
Onion, 1.
Oil, 1 tablespoonful.
Egg, 1.
Boiling water, 2 cups.
Granola.

Brown the onion in the oil, then add the minced nut foods and boiling water. Thicken with granola. Stir in the raw egg, and a little sage or thyme if desired. Salt to taste. Put in oiled pan and bake. Serve with gravy.

CREAM NUT LOAF

Dried bread crumbs, 2 cups.
Ground sweet corn, 1 cup.
Ground Brazil nuts, 1 cup.
Eggs, 2.
Sage.
Mashed peas, 1 cup.
Mashed potatoes, 1 cup.
Cream, ½ cup.
Salt.

Mix all thoroughly together, press in a deep bread-pan, and bake a nice brown. Serve with a sauce made of one part sweet cider and two parts grape juice, thickened with a little corn starch.

IMPERIAL NUT ROAST

Pea pulp, 1½ cups.
Chopped walnuts, 1½ cups.
Bread crumbs, 1 cup.
Sage.
Lentil pulp, 1½ cups.
Egg, 1.
Salt.
Milk to moisten.

Mix the peas, lentils, and walnuts with salt to taste. Put a layer in a deep bread-pan, then put a layer made of the crumbs, eggs, milk, sage, and salt. This should be just stiff enough to spread easily. Cover with the remaining pea and lentil mixture. Baste with cream, put in the oven, and brown.

WALNUT LOAF

Chopped walnut meats, ½ cup.
Egg, 1.
Boiling water, 2 cups.
Olive oil or butter, ½ tablespoonful.
Bread crumbs, 2 cups.
Salt to taste.

Mix walnut meats and crumbs together, pour over the boiling water, mix well, add the raw egg, butter, and salt, stir thoroughly, press into buttered bread-pan, and bake.

WALNUT ROAST

Granola, 2 cups.
Ground walnuts, 1 cup.
Milk or cream, 1 quart.
Eggs, 4.

Soak the granola in the milk or cream for ten minutes and add the walnuts, eggs, salt, and a dash of nutmeg. Mix the preparation well. Grease a baking-pan, turn in the mixture, and bake thirty-five to forty minutes.

CEREAL ROAST

Cream, 4 cups.
Nut meal, 1 cup.
Onion, chopped fine, 1.
Sage.
Gluten, ½ cup.
Bread crumbs, 1¼ cups.
Salt.

Mix all together and bake in a moderately hot oven.

NUT AND TOMATO ROAST

Celery, 1 root.
Granola, 1½ cups.
Eggs, 5.
Nuttolene, ½ pound.
Tomatoes, 2 cups.
Onions, 3.
Protose, ½ pound.

Chop the celery and onions fine, put into a sauce-pan with enough cooking oil to prevent burning, and cook until a rich brown, stirring occasionally. Add to this one quart of boiling water and the tomatoes. Boil for fifteen to twenty minutes. Then remove and strain as much as possible through a soup strainer. Take three and one-half cups of this gravy and mix with it the granola, eggs, and salt to taste. Have ready the protose and nuttolene cut into thin slices. Put in a layer of the granola mixture into a big baking-pan, then a layer of protose, then granola, then nuttolene, and so on until all is used, finishing with the granola mixture. Bake forty-five minutes or until a nice brown. Remove from the fire, let cool a little, turn out on a platter, and serve with the remaining gravy.

DRIED PEA CROQUETTES

Dried peas, 1½ cups.
Egg, 1.
Salt.
Olive oil, 2 teaspoonfuls.
Bread crumbs.

Cover the peas with water and soak overnight.
Drain and cook in fresh boiling water until tender.
Drain, press through a colander, add a little salt and
olive oil. Mix thoroughly and form into small rolls
about three inches long. Dip in beaten egg, roll in
bread crumbs, and bake in a quick oven. Serve with
tomato sauce.

CHICKEN CROQUETTES

Mashed potato, ½ cup.
Toasted bread crumbs, ½ cup.
Nut butter, ¼ cup.
Hard-boiled egg, chopped fine, 1.
Browned onion, ¼ cup
Sage, 1 teaspoonful.
Hot water, ½ cup.
Chopped walnuts, ¼ cup.
Minced nuttolene, 2 tablespoonfuls.
Beaten egg, 1.
Boiled rice, 1 cup.
Salt, 3 teaspoonfuls.

Mix all together and form into croquettes; dip into
beaten eggs and milk, roll in browned bread crumbs
which have been oiled or buttered, and bake.

HASHED PROTOSE CROQUETTES

Protose, 1 pound.
Butter, 1 tablespoonful.
Salt.
Potatoes, 1 pound.
Eggs, 4.
Mace.

Boil the potatoes, mash, add the minced protose, the yolk of three eggs, salt, and mace. Mix thoroughly, form into oblong croquettes; egg, crumb, and bake.

EGG MIXTURE FOR CROQUETTES, FILLETS, ETC.

Break an egg into a bowl or deep saucepan, break up with a fork, add a tablespoonful of hot water to soften the albumen of the egg, and mix till free from lumps, but do not beat in too much air. Dip the croquettes in the egg, roll in crumbs, and bake.

PROTOSE WITH BROWNED POTATOES

Peel and slice potatoes three-fourths of an inch thick. Cut protose in strips same thickness. Place in a pan two slices of potatoes and one of protose, and repeat same until the pan is full. Pour over this vegetable stock sufficient to cover. Bake in the oven till the potatoes are done and nicely browned.

NUT FRICASSEE WITH BROWNED SWEET POTATOES

Cut some nut food into half-inch cubes and pour over it a thick, brown or white gravy sufficient to cover well. Let it simmer about one hour. Peel and steam or boil potatoes until tender, but not over-done. Put them in a baking dish with a little butter or olive oil, salt, and bake in a quick oven until nicely browned. Serve with the fricassee.

FRIJOLES WITH PROTOSE MEXICANO

Mexican beans, ½ cup.
Vegetable stock, 1 cup.
Mace.
Diced protose, ¼ pound.
Strained tomatoes, 1 cup.
Salt.

Cook the beans in just enough water to prevent scorching. When done, have ready a stock made of the vegetable stock, tomatoes, mace, and salt. Pour over the beans, together with the protose, and let simmer for an hour or more.

FRICASSEE OF PROTOSE WITH POTATO

Serve a spoonful of nice white mashed potato on an empty platter; press a slice of broiled protose up against the potato, and serve with a spoonful of brown gravy. Garnish with parsley.

GREEN CORN AND TOMATO

Corn pulp, 3 cups.
Strained tomatoes, 1 cup.
Butter, 1 tablespoonful.
Salt.

Scrape the given amount of corn from the cob, add the tomatoes and butter, simmer until the corn is tender; salt, and serve as a vegetable.

Cold boiled corn cut from the cob may be substituted for the fresh corn, if desired.

MOCK CHICKEN RISSOLES

Protose, ½ pound.
Nuttolene, ½ pound.
Milk, ½ cup.
Mace.
Flour, 1 tablespoonful.
Butter, ¼ cup.
Salt.

Put the butter into a saucepan; when hot stir in the flour, and stir until brown; add the hot milk, salt, and mace, and let cook a few minutes. Chop the nut food fine and mix into the sauce. Have ready some tart shells made of rich pie paste; fill with the mixture. The sauce should be cool before adding the nut food.

NEW ENGLAND BOILED DINNER

Potatoes, 4½ cups.
Turnips, 1 cup.
Onions, 2 cups.
Carrots, 1¾ cups.
Cabbage, 2½ cups.

Cut the potatoes, carrots, and turnips in three-quarter inch cubes; slice the onions and cut the cabbage into pieces about one and one-half inch square. Boil the potatoes and onions together. The carrots, turnips and cabbage may also be cooked together in salted water. When all are done, mix together, and serve with slices of protose or other nut food that has been braized in a tomato or brown sauce.

NUT AND VEGETABLE STEW

Nuttolene, 1 cup.
Turnips, ¾ cup.
Chopped celery, ½ cup.
Bay leaf, 1.
Salt.
Carrots, 1½ cups.
Potatoes, 1½ cups.
Onion, small, 1.
Butter, 1 lump.

Put all on, except nuttolene and potatoes, and boil one hour. Then add potatoes and nuttolene and cook slowly until potatoes are done. Salt to taste. Thicken with a little flour, work smooth with a lump of butter. A little protose might also be added.

STEWED PROTOSE (SPANISH)

Butter, 1 tablespoonful.
Minced parsley, 1 tablespoonful.
Tomatoes, 4 cups.
Onions, 4.
Flour, 2 tablespoonfuls.
Protose, 1 pound.

Put the butter into a saucepan and add the sliced onion, minced parsley, and cook ten minutes. Then stir in the flour, mix well, and add the tomatoes. Stir well to free from lumps. Cover and cook twenty to thirty minutes. Slice the protose into small pieces and simmer in sauce ten minutes. Salt, and serve.

PROTOSE FRICASSEE

Tomatoes, 1 cup.
Minced parsley, 1 teaspoonful.
Protose, 1 pound.
Vegetable stock, 2 cups.
Mixed herbs, ½ teaspoonful.
Onion, 1.
Eggs (yolks), 2.

Mince the onion and braize in a little butter or olive oil five minutes; add the minced parsley strained tomatoes, mixed herbs, and vegetable broth. Bring to a boil and add the protose, cut into cubes or diamonds of one-half inch. Cook for a few minutes and thicken with a few spoonfuls of flour rubbed smooth in a little water. Salt to taste, and serve. Just before serving add the beaten yolks.

PROTOSE STEAK SMOTHERED IN ONIONS

Protose, ¾ pound.
Cooking oil, ½ cup.
Salt.
Onions, large, 6.
Vegetable stock, 2 cups.

Cut the protose into twelve slices, lay half of them in an oiled baking-pan; have the onions sliced and lightly browned in the oil. Cook half of the onions over the protose, then put on the rest of the protose, then the remainder of the onions, pouring the vegetable stock over all. Salt to taste. Bake until the stock is reduced to a rich brown gravy.

PROTOSE SMOTHERED WITH TOMATOES

Protose, ¾ pound.
Butter, ½ cup.
Salt.
Tomatoes, 12.
Sugar, 2 tablespoonfuls.
Celery salt.

Cut protose into twelve slices and cut each tomato in half. Put one slice of tomato in a baking-pan; on this put a slice of the protose, then a slice of tomato on top, and so on, making twelve orders in all. Chop the butter in little pieces and sprinkle over, also the salt and celery salt. Cover and bake until the tomato is nearly done. Then remove the cover and brown very lightly. Serve two slices to each person, garnished with parsley.

PROTOSE POT ROAST

Protose, ¾ pound.
Strained tomatoes, 1 cup.
Vegetable soup stock, 2 cups.
Salt to taste.

Mix the vegetable stock with the strained tomatoes, salt to taste, and pour over the protose, which has been sliced and placed in a baking-pan. Bake one hour.

BRAIZED PROTOSE AND CABBAGE

Braize protose according to the recipe, and serve with boiled cabbage.

PROTOSE STEAK WITH POTATOES SMOTH-ERED IN ONIONS

By putting a layer of sliced raw potatoes in the bottom of the pan and covering with the protose, onions, and stock, we have protose steak and potatoes smothered with onions.

PROTOSE PILAU

Water, ¾ pint.
Rice, cooked, 1 cup.
Butter, 1 teaspoonful.
Protose, ½ inch cubes, ¼ pound.
Minced onion, 1 tablespoonful.

Let simmer ten or fifteen minutes; thicken with browned flour, two heaping teaspoonfuls, mixed with strained tomatoes to consistency to pour easily. Salt and celery salt to taste.

PROTOSE PATTIES (PLAIN)

Protose, 1 pound.
Salt.
Cream, 3 tablespoonfuls.
Eggs, 2.
Bread crumbs.

Thoroughly crush the protose and mix with the salt and one egg. Form into patties, roll in egg and cream, then in bread crumbs. Bake in greased pan till lightly browned. If desired, the crumbs may be slightly moistened with cream.

BRAIZED PROTOSE

Protose, 12 slices.
Vegetable stock, No. 2, 3 cups.
Sage.
Minced onion, medium size, 1.
Butter.

Butter a deep pan and sprinkle with the minced onion and sage. On this lay the slices of protose, cut a little less than half an inch thick. Cover the pan and put into the oven to brown, turning the protose once, and watching carefully that the onions do not burn. Remove from the oven and cover with the vegetable stock. Cover and return to the oven, and bake until the stock is reduced to a thick, brown gravy.

PROTOSE CUTLETS WITH MASHED POTATO

Protose, ½ pound.
Milk, 1 cup.
Brown sauce.
Egg, 1.
Granose flakes.

Cut protose into six slices as for protose steak. Dip in beaten egg and milk, and roll in granose flakes. Do this the second time, and bake in brown sauce about thirty minutes. Serve with mashed potato.

NUT LISBON STEAK

Protose, 6 large slices.
Brown gravy, 3 cups.

Broil or fry the protose a nice brown (but do not burn) and drop into the gravy (any good brown gravy will do); let simmer an hour or two. Serve hot with a spoonful of the gravy.

More protose may be used if desired.

PROTOSE AND TOMATO

Protose, 6 large slices.
Tomato, cooked and strained, 2 cups
Corn starch, 1 teaspoonful.
Salt to taste.

Cut the protose in rather thick slices and lay in a flat baking-pan (one about two inches deep will answer nicely); boil the tomatoes and thicken with the corn starch; add the salt, and pour over the protose. Bake slowly in a moderate oven. Do not bake too dry. The protose should be nice and juicy with the tomatoes when done. The corn starch may be omitted if desired.

BAKED PROTOSE WITH MACARONI

Macaroni (not cooked), 1½ cups.
Oil, 1 tablespoonful.
Flour, ⅓ cup.
Salt.
Minced protose, 1 cup.
Minced onion, medium size, 1.
Milk, 2 cups.

Break the protose in one-inch lengths. Drop in three quarts of boiling water, previously salted. Boil from one-half to three-quarters hour, turn into colander, and pour cold water over it. Drain and turn into baking-pan.

SAUCE

Put the oil in a stew-pan, add the onion, braize till nicely browned, then add the flour, and stir until brown. Add the milk, then the protose. Season with salt. Pour this sauce over the macaroni and sprinkle with bread crumbs. Bake in a moderate oven till brown.

FRIZZLED PROTOSE IN EGGS

Protose, 1 pound.
Eggs, 8.
Olive oil.

Cut the protose into small, thin, narrow strips; put into a frying-pan with a little olive oil, and when hot pour the well-beaten eggs over it, stirring constantly, until the eggs are set. Serve hot on toast.

ESCALLOPED PROTOSE

Protose, 1 pound.
Bread crumbs, ¾ cup.
Potatoes, medium size, 4.
Brown sauce, sufficient to cover.

Slice one-half the potatoes in a baking dish, sprinkle one-half the bread crumbs over them; on the crumbs put half the protose cut into thin slices; pour over some of the gravy to moisten. Add the remainder of the ingredients in the same manner, ma-

king two layers. There should be sufficient gravy
to cover and cook the potatoes and protose.

EGGPLANT BAKED WITH PROTOSE

Eggplant, medium size, 2.
Chopped onion, large, 1.
Salt.
Protose, ¾ pound.
Vegetable stock.

Peel and slice the eggplant in one-fourth inch
slices, and cut the protose into twelve slices. Put
a layer of the eggplant in an oiled pan, then a layer
of protose, and sprinkle part of the onion over all.
Make another layer with the remainder and cover
with vegetable stock. Salt to taste, cover, and bake.
Tomato may be used in place of the stock if desired.

PROTOSE JAMBALAYA

Butter, 1 tablespoonful.
Minced onion, 1.
Minced garlic, small, 1.
Flour, 1 tablespoonful.
Tomatoes, 1½ cups.
Vegetable stock, 1½ quarts.
Rice, 1 cup.
Minced protose, ¾ pound.
Minced celery, ¼ cup.
Salt, mace, and bay leaves.

Put the butter into a saucepan, heat, add the
onion and garlic, and brown, then add the flour
and brown, add the tomato, and cook a few minutes,
stirring to prevent flour from lumping. When nice

and brown, add vegetable stock and the seasoning; boil until the ingredients are well blended; add the rice and boil till the rice is tender, stirring often. To this add the minced protose that has been heated in a covered dish in the oven.   Mix and serve.

RAGOUT OF PROTOSE

Protose cut in irregular pieces, 1 pound.
Hot water, 4 cups.
Browned flour, 1 tablespoonful.
Celery salt.
Strained tomatoes, 1½ cups.
White flour, 1 tablespoonful.
Salt.

Put all together, except the flour, and let simmer thirty or forty minutes, adding enough boiling water from time to time to keep the original quantity. Thicken with the flour, and serve.

PROTOSE CUTLETS

(1) Protose, minced, 1 pound.
Season with
Salt.
Lemon juice.
Sage.
Add a little
Chopped parsley.
Make a heavy white sauce with
(2) Flour, 2 tablespoonfuls.
Milk, ¾ cup.
If desired, flour may be rubbed with
Butter, 1 tablespoonful.
Add salt to taste.

Mix 1 thoroughly with 2. When cool, make into patties, cutlets, or croquettes. Dip into beaten egg, roll in bread crumbs that have been moistened with melted butter, and brown in the oven.

PROTOSE CHARTREUSE

Vegetable stock, 2 cups.
Egg, 1.
Salt.
Protose, ½ pound.
Rice, cooked, 1 quart.
Bread crumbs, sufficient to thicken.

To the stock add the protose, bread crumbs, the egg unbeaten, and salt. Mix thoroughly. Line a baking-pan with part of the rice, and fill in the center with the protose mixture; cover with the rest of the rice, and press down gently. Bake, and serve with browned sauce.

PROTOSE STEAK

Split a pound of protose in two lengthwise, and cut into as many slices as needed. Broil in a pan, and serve with brown sauce.

PROTOSE STEAK A LA TARTARE

Minced protose, 1 pound.
Butter, 1 tablespoonful.
Mayonnaise, 3 tablespoonfuls.
Onion, 1.
Eggs, 6.
Onions and olives mixed, to garnish.

Put the butter in a saucepan and set on the range. When hot, add the onion and cook until brown; add the minced protose, a pinch of salt, and mix. Form into balls, making a depression in each ball, and drop an egg yolk in each depression. Bake until the eggs are done. Chop the onions and olives, add the mayonnaise, and use as a garnish.

PROTOSE OR NUTTOLENE CUTLETS

Protose or nuttolene, 6 slices, each large enough
    for a cutlet.
Eggs, 3.
Cream or rich milk, 2 cups.
Bread crumbs, buttered, 1½ cups.
Salt.

Beat the eggs, add the milk and salt, dip the slices of nut food in this, and then in the buttered bread crumbs, and lay in a greased baking-pan. Place the remaining bread crumbs with the milk, add salt, and pour over the cutlets. If not enough to cover, a little milk may be added. Put into the oven and bake till the mixture sets, or it may be placed on the range, and when one side is browned turn and brown the other side.

GOLDEN NUT CHARTREUSE

Vegetable stock, 2 cups.
Corn meal mush, 1 quart.
Bread crumbs.
Egg, 1.
Protose, or other nut food, ½ pound.
Salt.

Make the filling same as for protose chartreuse; line the pan with the mush, put in the filling, and cover with mush. Bake, and when cold cut into slices, egg, crumb, and bake. Serve with gravy.

LENTIL HASH

Lentils, 1 cup.
Potatoes, medium size, 2
Rice, 2 tablespoonfuls.
Egg, 1.
Onion, large, 1.
Tomato, 1.
Cooking oil, ¼ cup.
Garlic, small piece.

Boil the lentil, onion, tomato, potatoes, and rice together till soft; chop very fine and add the cooking oil, egg, and a very small piece of garlic, and salt to taste. Put into oiled pan and bake until brown.

LENTIL FRITTERS

Lentils, 1 cup.
Rich milk, ¼ cup.
Egg, 1.
Butter, 1 tablespoonful.
Flour, ¾ cup.

Cook lentils until tender, drain, press through a colander, add the milk, butter, flour, salt, and beaten yolk. Mix thoroughly and add the stiffly-beaten white. Drop in spoonfuls on oiled griddle and brown on both sides, or bake in the oven. Garnish with parsley, and serve with marmalade or apple sauce.

WALNUT LENTIL PATTIES

Cooked lentils, 2 cups.
Eggs, 2.
Chopped walnuts, ¾ cup.
Granola, or bread crumbs.

Rub the lentils through a colander and add the chopped walnut meats, one egg, and a pinch of salt. Thicken with bread crumbs or granola. Form into patties, roll in egg and buttered crumbs, and bake. Serve with gravy.

LENTIL PATTIES ON MACARONI

Lentils, 1 cup.
Eggs, 2.
Chopped parsley, 1 teaspoonful.
Minced onion, 2 tablespoonfuls.
Olive oil, 2 tablespoonfuls.
Bread crumbs.

Cook the lentils until tender and put through a colander. To this pulp add the rest of the ingredients, using sufficient bread crumbs to make stiff enough to form into patties. Dip the patties in egg and crumbs. Brown in the oven. Serve on a platter with creamed macaroni.

WALNUT LENTILS

Lentils, 1½ cups.
Walnuts, 1 cup.
Butter.

Cook the lentils in six cups of water until quite tender and the water almost dried away. Press the

lentils through a soup strainer. Grind the walnut
meats and add to the lentils. Add a little butter and
salt to taste.

LENTIL ROAST

Lentils, 1½ cups.
Butter, 1 tablespoonful.
Granola, 1 cup.
Eggs, 2.
Onion, small, 1.
Mixed herbs, 1 teaspoonful.
Ground walnuts, 1 cup.
Salt.

Cook the lentils in sufficient water to prevent burning. When tender, add the sliced onion, butter,
mixed herbs, and salt to taste. Cook with the pot
closely covered for twenty-five to thirty minutes
longer.

Remove from fire, drain, press through a colander,
and add the granola, ground walnuts, and eggs.
Mix well, press into a baking pan, and bake forty-
five minutes or until nicely browned.

LENTIL NUT ROAST

Lentil pulp, 2 cups.
Egg, 1.
Toasted bread crumbs or granola.
Nut butter, ½ cup.
Dairy butter, 2 teaspoonfuls.

Emulsify the nut butter in enough water to mix
easily. Mix all together and thicken with toasted
bread crumbs or granola. Salt to taste. Put in

oiled pan and bake. Serve with gravy. A little thyme or sage may be used if desired.

RICE MOLD

Rice, 1 cup.
Milk, ⅔ cup
Lemon or vanilla flavoring.
Egg, 1.
Sugar, 2 tablespoonfuls.
Stewed fruit.

Wash clean and boil the rice in two quarts of water until done. Drain off the water well. Add, while hot, a custard made of the egg, milk, and sugar. Flavor with lemon or vanilla. Form into molds, and serve with stewed prunes, peaches, or any other kind of fruit.

RICE AND BANANA COMPOTE

Rice, ¾ cup.
Milk, 3 cups.
Vanilla.
Bananas, 6.
Sugar.

Bring the milk to a boil, thicken with corn starch or flour, and add sugar to taste. Simmer the bananas in this sauce for half an hour. Add vanilla.

Rice for bananas: Cook the rice in two and one-fourth cups of water in a double boiler till done. The rice should be soft and each grain standing out separate when done. Make a layer of the rice, and serve the bananas on it.

RICE AND EGG SCRAMBLE

Rice, 2 cups.
Eggs, 4.
Milk, 4 cups.

Thoroughly wash the rice and boil in salted water until tender and drain. Scramble the eggs in the milk, add salt when nearly done, mix with the rice, and serve hot.

SPANISH RICE

Rice, 1 cup.
Garlic, medium size, ½.
Bay leaf, 1.
Minced celery, 1 stalk.
Tomatoes, 2 cups.
Minced onion, small, 1.
Oil, 2 tablespoonfuls.
Mace, ½ teaspoonful.
Flour, 2 tablespoonfuls.
Salt.

Boil the rice until about half done, drain, and finish cooking in the following sauce:—

Put the oil in a saucepan, add all the other ingredients except the tomato and flour; set over the fire and stir occasionally, to prevent burning, until brown. Then add the flour and stir till brown. Add the tomato, let cook a few minutes, strain, and add to the rice.

CORN FRITTERS

Green corn pulp, 1 pint.
Milk, 4 tablespoonfuls.
Flour, ½ cup.
Eggs, 4.

Mix the corn, milk, flour, and yolks of the eggs together thoroughly. Then fold in the well-beaten whites of the eggs, and fry by spoonfuls.

PROTOSE AND RICE CHOWDER

Protose, ½ pound.
Rice, cooked, 1 cup.
Potatoes, ½ pound.
Butter, 1 tablespoonful.
Vegetable stock, 1 cup.
Bread, ¼ loaf.
Cream, or milk, 1 cup.
Salt and mace to taste.

Put the butter in a deep dish, melt, then add a layer of the protose, sliced quite thin, then sprinkle with mace, salt, and bits of butter. Then add a layer of the sliced potatoes, sprinkle with part of the rice, then a layer of bread, then more salt, bits of butter, and minced onion. Add the remainder in the same order, and pour over all one cup of hot vegetable stock. Cover, set on range, and let simmer one-half hour, then pour over all one cup of hot cream or milk, and serve.

NOODLES

Butter, 1 tablespoonful.
Salt, ¼ teaspoonful.
Eggs, 2.
Flour, to make a very stiff dough.

Whip the egg until light, add the salt, and work in the flour, making a smooth, stiff dough. Roll out thin, in a long narrow strip, sprinkle with flour to

7

prevent sticking, and roll up into a long roll, rolling crosswise. Then with a sharp knife cut into very thin slices and drop into boiling salted water. Cook about twenty minutes. Drain, pour over the melted butter, and serve hot.

VEGETABLE OYSTER A L'ITALIENNE

Take macaroni broken into one-inch lengths, and boiled until tender, and vegetable oyster which has been parboiled twenty minutes, and put in alternate layers in a baking-pan. Pour over this a sauce made from both of the liquors (macaroni and vegetable oyster) thickened with the yolks of the eggs. Sprinkle with granola and bake until browned.

GREEN CORN CHOWDER (NEW ENGLAND STYLE)

Corn pulp, fresh cut from the cob, 2½ cups.
Diced protose, 1 cup.
Vegetable stock, 1 cup.
Parsley, chopped, 1 tablespoonful.
Bread crumbs.
Minced onion, medium size, 1.
Sliced potatoes, 2 cups.
Oil, 2 tablespoonfuls.
Salt.

Brown the onion in the oil, and add the protose and vegetable stock. When thoroughly heated, add corn pulp, mix all together, heat up well, and salt. Put the sliced potatoes in cold water, drain, and put into a pan of flour; shake the pan so as to cover the potatoes with flour. Put half of the potatoes in a layer in the bottom of a baking-pan, cover with half the corn and protose mixture, sprinkle with bread crumbs and part of the parsley. In the same manner add the remainder of the potatoes and mixture. Moisten with stock and bake until the potatoes are done.

SQUASH FRITTERS

Mashed summer squash, 2 cups.
Butter, 1 heaping tablespoonful.
Sugar, 1 tablespoonful.
Salt, ½ teaspoonful.
Rich milk, ½ cup.
Flour, 1 cup.
Eggs, 2.

Mix thoroughly the squash, butter, milk, flour sugar, salt, and beaten yolks. Then fold in the stiffly-beaten whites. Brown on a griddle.

BEAN CROQUETTES

Navy beans, 1 cup.
Olive oil, 1 tablespoonful.
Bread crumbs.
Salt, 1 level teaspoonful.
Beaten egg, 1.

Cover beans with water, soak overnight, drain, and cook in fresh boiling water until tender, or about an hour. Drain, press through a colander, add salt and olive oil. Mix thoroughly and roll into cylinder-shaped croquettes; dip into beaten egg, roll in bread crumbs and bake in moderate oven. Serve with tomato sauce.

SCOTCH PEA LOAF

Scotch pea pulp, 1½ cups.
Egg, 1.
Poultry dressing or sage.
Nut food, 1 pound.
Butter, 2 teaspoonfuls.

Stir all together, or thicken with toasted bread crumbs or granola; bake. Serve with gravy.

BEAN AND NUT LOAF

White beans, 1 cup.
Onion, ¼ cup.
Sage.
Toasted bread crumbs or granola.
Chopped walnuts, 1 cup.
Egg, 1.
Salt.

Thoroughly wash the beans and soak overnight. Boil thoroughly, and when done rub through a colander. Add the chopped walnuts, egg, onion braized in oil, sage, and salt to taste. Thicken with granola or toasted bread crumbs. Put into an oiled pan and bake. Serve with gravy.

CARROT SOUFFLE

Mashed carrots, 1½ cups.
Rich milk, 1 cup.
Toasted bread crumbs, or granola, 1½ cups.
Braized onion, 1 tablespoonful.
Nutmeg, 1 level teaspoonful.
Yolks of eggs, 3.

Beat the whites of the eggs very stiff and fold into the above mixture. Put into oiled pan, and bake in moderate oven.

OKRA GUMBO (VEGETARIAN STYLE)

Ripe tomatoes, 2 cups.
Water, 1½ quarts.
Diced nuttolene, ¼ pound.
Onion, medium size, 1.
Sliced okra, 2 cups.
Diced protose, ½ pound.
Butter, 1 tablespoonful.
Rice, boiled, 1 cup.
Salt, celery salt, mace.
Watercress, parsley.

Cook the tomatoes and okra in the water. Brown the onion in the butter, add the protose and nuttolene with the seasoning; brown all together a few minutes; then add the tomato and okra; let all simmer for two hours. Serve on platters on tablespoonful of boiled rice. Garnish with the parsley or cress.

BAKED POT PIE

Protose, 1 pound.
Carrots, 1½ cups.
Strained tomato, 1 cup.
Thyme.
Potatoes, 2 cups.
Minced onion, ½ cup.
Chopped parsley.

Cook the carrots about one hour, then add potatoes, onions, protose, and a little chopped parsley. Simmer in just enough water to keep from burning until potatoes are done. Season with thyme and salt to taste. Put in an oiled pan and cover with a rich pie paste. Bake thirty to forty minutes in a moderate oven.

BAKED EGGPLANT A LA CREME

Eggplant, 6 slices.
Milk, 3 cups.
Butter.
Toasted bread crumbs, ½ cup.
Salt, 2 teaspoonfuls.

Peel the eggplant and cut in slices about three-fourths of an inch thick. Place slices in a pan and cover with sifted toasted bread crumbs or sifted granola. Pour over this the milk; add salt and small piece of butter, and bake. If it becomes too dry, add a little more milk.

MOCK CHICKEN PIE

Boiled potatoes, 4 cups.
Nuttolene, ½ pound.
Eggs, 2.
Pie crust.
Protose, ½ pound.
Milk, 1 cup.
Chopped onion and parsley.
Nut gravy.

Put into an oiled baking-pan a layer of the thinly-sliced boiled potato, and over this a layer of nuttolene cut into thin slices. Sprinkle on a little chopped onion and parsley, then a layer of sliced protose. Pour over the nut gravy and let set five minutes. Cover this with the pie crust and bake till done.

GREEN CORN NUT PIE

Corn mixture.
    Corn ground, 2 cans.
    Rich milk, 1 cup.
    Flour, ¾ cup.
    Beaten eggs, 2.
    Salt to taste.
Nut mixture.
    Minced onion, 1.
    Chopped celery, ¼ cup.
Braize in a little butter or oil. Add
    Water, 1 cup.
    Strained tomatoes, ½ cup.
    Minced nuttolene or protose, ¾ cup.

Add to this sufficient bread crumbs to make a batter that will spread easily. Oil a baking-pan, and cover the bottom with one-half of the corn mixture, then put in the nut food mixture and the remainder of the corn to top. Bake till nicely browned.

VEGETABLE OYSTER PIE

    Vegetable oysters, 1 quart.
    Potatoes, 1 cup.
    Cream sauce, 2½ cups.
    Pie paste sufficient to cover.
    Chopped parsley, 1 teaspoonful.
    Parsnips, 1 cup.
    Salt.

Boil the vegetables separately until tender; then mix with the other ingredients and put in a shallow baking-pan. Cover with the pie paste and bake a light brown. Serve hot.

VERMICELLI NUT PIE

Nuttolene, ½ pound.
Vermicelli, 2 cups.
Salt.
Rich milk, 4 cups.
Eggs, 2.

Cook the nuttolene ten minutes in two cups of rich milk, then rub through a strainer. Flavor with celery salt. Cook the vermicelli fifteen minutes, strain, and pour over it while in the strainer two quarts of cold water. When it is well drained, line the bottom of a pie dish with one-half of it. Pour over it the puree of nuttolene and cover with the other half of the vermicelli. Make a custard of two eggs, two cups of milk, and a teaspoonful of salt. Turn this custard over the pie, and with a fork make an impression all over, to permit the custard to run through. Sprinkle a few bread crumbs over it, and bake in a quick oven thirty minutes. Serve with or without sauce.

NUT AND VEGETABLE PIE

Minced onion, 1 cup.
Minced parsley, ½ cup.

Brown and add

Mashed carrots, 2 cups.
Mashed potatoes, 2 cups.
Nut food, 1 pound.
Eggs, 2.
Salt to taste and put in oiled pan. Pour over this

a mixture made by beating one egg in one cup milk, and bake in a moderate oven till it is nicely browned.

TOMATO PIE

Tomatoes, 6.
Chopped parsley.
Salt.
Cooking oil, ⅓ cup.
Pie paste.

Peel and slice the tomatoes and place in a small baking-pan. On top of this put some chopped parsley, a pinch of salt, and cooking oil. Cover with thin pie paste and bake.

BOILED MACARONI (PLAIN)

Put two cups of macaroni, broken into inch lengths, into a saucepan, cover with plenty of boiling water, salted, and boil till tender, or about thirty minutes. Stir gently once or twice, to prevent sticking to the bottom. Add enough cold water to stop boiling and let it come to a boil again. Drain in a colander. Boiled macaroni may be served with a gravy or fruit sauce.

MACARONI A L'ITALIENNE

Macaroni, raw, 1 cup.
Corn meal, 2 tablespoonfuls.
Grated onion, 2 tablespoonfuls.
Salt to taste.
Milk or cream, 2 cups.
Tomatoes, cooked and strained, 1 cup.

Break the macaroni into one-inch lengths; boil in

salted water till done; drain. While the macaroni is
cooking, boil the milk and thicken with the corn
meal. When thoroughly cooked, add the tomatoes,
onions, and salt. Pour this dressing over the macaroni, and serve hot.

MACARONI AND KORNLET

Macaroni, raw, 1 cup.
Cream or rich milk, ¾ cup.
Kornlet, ¾ cup.
Salt to taste.

Break the macaroni in one-inch lengths and boil
in salted water till tender. Drain, add the kornlet,
cream, and salt. Mix thoroughly, spread in a baking-pan, and bake a light brown. There should be
enough kornlet and cream to cover the macaroni
smoothly, and it should not be too moist when done.

MACARONI WITH TOMATO SAUCE

Macaroni, raw, 1 cup.
Flour, 1 tablespoonful.
Cream, ½ cup.
Tomatoes, stewed and strained, 2 cups.
Salt to taste.

Break the macaroni into one-inch lengths and boil
in salted water till thoroughly done. Boil tomatoes
and thicken with flour, rubbed smooth in a little
water. Add the cream, which should be hot, and
salt to taste. Drain the macaroni, pour the sauce
over, mix well, and serve. The cream may be
omitted if preferred.

MACARONI CUTLETS

Macaroni, raw, 1 cup.
Flour, 2 heaping tablespoonfuls.
Minced protose, 1 cup.
Salt to taste.
Milk, 1 cup.
Egg, 1.
Bread crumbs.

Boil the macaroni in salted water till done, drain, and chop fine. Boil the milk and thicken with the flour; stir in the well-beaten egg; beat thoroughly. Add the macaroni, protose, and salt, and make stiff with the bread crumbs, so that it can be made into cutlets. Make into any shape desired. Put into an oiled pan and bake till nicely browned. Serve with tomato or cream sauce.

CREAMED MACARONI

Rich milk, 2 cups.
Flour, 2 large tablespoonfuls.
Salt.
Macaroni, 1 cup.
Butter.

Boil the macaroni and put it into a gravy made of the milk, flour, butter, and salt. Mix well, and serve.

MACARONI IN CREAM

Macaroni, 2½ cups.
Milk, 4 cups.
Egg yolk, 1.
Cream, 1 cup.

Cook the macaroni in plenty of boiling water
thirty minutes. Turn off the water and wash the
macaroni by pouring two or three quarts of cold
water over it. Return the macaroni to the saucepan
and add the boiling milk. Remove to a cool part of
the stove and cook for thirty minutes. Before serving, add the beaten yolk and the boiling cream.
Shake the pot to mix the egg with the macaroni.
Stir as little as possible. Salt to taste.

EGG MACARONI

Macaroni, 1½ cups.
Eggs, hard-boiled, 3.
Cream gravy, 2 cups.
Bread crumbs.

Break macaroni into one-inch lengths and boil in
salted water till tender. Drain and wash with cold
water. Put into a baking dish and sprinkle over it
the hard-boiled eggs chopped fine. Stir into cream
gravy, made from rich milk, sprinkle top with bread
crumbs. Bake until nicely browned.

BAKED MACARONI WITH EGG SAUCE

Macaroni, 2 cups.
Milk, 3 cups.
Granola.
Eggs, 4.
Salt, 1 tablespoonful.

Break the macaroni into inch lengths and boil in
salted water thirty to thirty-five minutes. Drain,
turn it into a deep pan. Pour over this a custard
made with the milk, beaten eggs, and salt. Sprinkle

with granola on top, and bake in a moderate oven thirty minutes.

MACARONI WITH APPLE

Butter a deep baking-dish and put in a layer of mashed and sweetened apple sauce. Grate a little nutmeg over and add a layer of cooked macaroni. Repeat till the dish is full, finishing with the apple sauce. Bake till the apples are slightly browned. Serve with sweetened cream, seasoned with nutmeg. May be served as a dessert.

MACARONI AND CHEESE (VEGETARIAN STYLE NO. 1)

Macaroni, 2½ cups.
Egg sauce, 1 cup.
Sour cream, ½ cup.
Granola.

Break the macaroni into inch lengths and boil in salted water until tender. Drain and mix in a little granola. Add the sour cream or thick sour milk and about one cup of egg sauce. (See egg sauce recipe, page 156.) Season to taste and bake.

MACARONI AND CHEESE (VEGETARIAN STYLE NO. 2)

Macaroni, 2½ cups.
Cottage cheese, 1¼ cups.
Milk.
Butter, 1 tablespoonful.
Bread crumbs.

Break the macaroni and cook in salted water until about half done. Drain and pour over it enough milk to cover, and simmer until done. Add the cottage cheese and butter and mix thoroughly. Pour into baking-pan, sprinkle with bread crumbs, and bake.

MACARONI WITH GRANOLA

Macaroni, raw, 2 cups.
Granola, ½ cup.
Salt to taste.
Cream sauce, 2½ cups.
Butter, 1 tablespoonful.

Cook the macaroni till tender; drain, put one-half in a baking-pan, sprinkle on one-half of the granola, and cover with one-half of the gravy. Repeat with the remainder, making two layers. Bake until nicely browned.

MACARONI CROQUETTES

Macaroni, raw, 2 cups.
Butter, 1 tablespoonful.
Egg yolks, 2.
Milk, 1 cup.
Flour, 2 tablespoonfuls.
Salt to taste.

Boil the macaroni in salted water until tender, drain, and chop fine. Heat the milk; when boiling, add the butter and flour, that have been rubbed together until smooth; stir until thick, remove from the range, and stir in quickly the beaten yolks of the eggs. Mix this sauce with the macaroni, season with salt, turn out into a flat pan, and let cool.

When cold, form into croquettes, egg, crumb, and bake.

MACARONI NEAPOLITAINE

Vegetable stock, 3 cups.
Diced protose, ½ pound.
Macaroni, raw, 1 cup.
Salt to taste.

Cook the macaroni, drain, and add the rest of the ingredients. Let simmer thirty minutes. Serve.

MACARONI (SPANISH STYLE)

Macaroni, 2 cups.
Onion, 1.
Cream sauce, 2 cups.
Salt to taste.
Eggs, 3.
Parsley, chopped fine, 1 teaspoonful.
Dash of nutmeg.

Cook the macaroni in salted water, drain, and chop fine; have the eggs boiled hard and chopped fine, and the onions grated. Mix all together, sprinkle with toasted bread crumbs, and brown in the oven. Serve with tomato or Chili sauce.

MACARONI WITH TOMATO

Stewed tomatoes, 2 cups.
Butter, 2 tablespoonfuls.
Hard-boiled eggs, grated or rubbed through a
    colander, 1 cup.
Salt.
Vegetable stock, 2 cups.
Macaroni, 2 cups.

Boil the macaroni till tender, drain, and add the
stock and tomatoes not strained (they should be
put on a sieve and allowed to drain, as the stock
will afford sufficient liquid), but chopped, and there
should not be enough of them to allow the tomato
taste to predominate. Now add to this the hard-
boiled eggs, grated or rubbed through a colander.
Mix all together, and add a little salt. Pour into
a baking-pan about four inches deep, and bake until
the mixture is thick. A few lumps of butter
sprinkled over the top as it goes to the oven is an
improvement.

SCALLOPED MACARONI WITH VEGE-
TABLE OYSTERS

Vegetable oysters, peeled and sliced, 2 cups.
Macaroni, 1 cup.
Rich milk, 2 cups.
Butter, 1 tablespoonful.
Salt.
Eggs, 2.
Flour, 2 tablespoonfuls.
Bread crumbs.

Boil the macaroni and vegetable oysters separately, and drain. Then place same in alternate layers in a pan. Pour over this a gravy made of the
milk, flour, eggs, butter, and salt. Stir carefully so
as to get the gravy mixed through thoroughly.
Sprinkle a few bread crumbs on top and bake in a
quick oven till nicely browned.

SPAGHETTI IN TOMATO SAUCE

Broken spaghetti, 2 cups.
Flour, 2 tablespoonfuls.
Bay leaves, 2.
Onion, minced, 1.
Tomatoes, 4 cups.

Break the spaghetti into small pieces and boil until well done. Pour over this tomato sauce, made as follows: Brown the minced onion in a little oil, stir in the flour, and add tomatoes, bay leaves, and salt to taste. Let boil, and strain.

PROTOSE HASH

Protose, 1½ cups.
Cold boiled or baked potatoes, 2 cups.
Oil.
Chopped onions, large, 2.
Salt.
Sage.

Put all together in a pan, pour over a little cooking oil, and set on the stove. When it begins to brown, stir up with a thin knife occasionally until well browned.

VEGETARIAN HAMBURGER STEAK

Protose, 1 pound.
Sage, ½ teaspoonful.
Eggs, 2.
Nuttolene, ½ pound.
Grated onion, 1 tablespoonful.
Granose biscuits, powdered fine, 2.

Mix thoroughly, form into patties, and fry. Serve with tomato sauce.

8

VEGETARIAN HAMBURGER STEAK WITH MACARONI

Serve vegetarian hamburger steak with macaroni and a little brown sauce.

VEGETARIAN SAUSAGE

Boiled rice, 3 cups.
Grated onion, 6 teaspoonfuls.
Protose, 1 pound.
Salt, 1½ teaspoonfuls.
Oil, 3 tablespoonfuls.
Sage, 6 teaspoonfuls.
Egg, 1.

Form into patties, and roll in gluten or browned flour, and bake in a frying-pan. If browned in the oven, put a small piece of butter on top of each.

BAKED STUFFED TOMATOES

Tomatoes, medium sized, 6.
Chopped protose, ½ pound.
Sage, ½ teaspoonful.
Chopped parsley.
Toasted bread crumbs, 8 to 12 tablespoonfuls.
Chopped onion, 1 tablespoonful.
Salt, 1 teaspoonful.

Take out the inside of the tomatoes and mix with this the bread crumbs. Then add the other ingredients, and fill the tomatoes, piling mixture up on top. Place small piece of butter on each, and bake in a hot oven, until the tomatoes are cooked. When nearly done, sprinkle chopped parsley over the top.

VEGETABLES

VEGETABLES

The term "vegetable," as here used, is applied to such plants (grains, nuts, and fruits excepted) as are cultivated and used for food. The use of a large variety of vegetables in our food assists in promoting good health. To get the best results, they should be judiciously combined with nuts, fruits, and grains. Green vegetables are rich in potash salts and other minerals necessary to the system, and in such a form as to be easily assimilated.

Starchy vegetables, as potatoes, supply energy and heat, and give necessary bulk to the food. Peas, beans, and lentils contain a large amount of proteid, used in building and repairing tissue, and are therefore used in place of meat. For weak stomachs they are more easily digested in the form of purees and soups, with the outer indigestible covering removed. All vegetables should be fresh; for in spite of all that may be said to the contrary, all vegetables, whether roots, leaves, or any other kind, begin to lose bulk and flavor as soon as removed from the ground. The kind that suffer least in this respect are beets, potatoes, carrots, etc. Those which are most easily affected are cabbage, lettuce, celery, asparagus, etc.

Vegetables that have been touched with the frost should be kept in a perfectly dark place for some days. The frost is then drawn out slowly, and the vegetables are not so liable to rot.

GENERAL DIRECTIONS FOR VEGETABLES

Fresh green vegetables should be cooked as soon after being gathered as possible. Those containing sugar, as corn and peas, lose some of their sweetness by standing. Wash thoroughly in cold water, but unless wilted do not soak. It is better not to prepare fresh green vegetables until they are needed; but if they must be prepared some time before cooking, cover with cold water.

Most vegetables should be put into fresh, rapidly-boiling water, and if cooked in uncovered vessels, they will retain a better color, as high heat destroys their color. In no instance permit them to steep in the warm water, as this toughens them, and in some instances destroys both color and flavor.

The salt hardens the water, and also sets the color in the vegetable. For peas and beans do not add salt to the water until they are nearly done, as they do not boil tender so readily in hard water.

Corn should not be boiled in salt water, as the salt hardens the outer covering of skin and makes it tough. Cook the vegetables rapidly till perfectly tender, but no longer. If vegetables are cooked too long, flavor, color, and appearance are all impaired. To judge when done, watch carefully, and test by piercing with a fork. The time required to cook a vegetable varies with its age and freshness;

therefore, the time tables given for cooking serve only as approximate guides.

Delicate vegetables, as green peas, shelled beans, celery, etc., should be cooked in as little water as possible, toward the last the water being allowed to boil away till there is just enough left to moisten. In this manner all the desirable soluble matter that may have been drawn out in cooking is saved.

Strongly flavored vegetables, as cabbage, onions, etc., should be cooked in a generous quantity of water, and the water in which onions are cooked may be changed one or more times.

The general rule for seasoning vegetables is as follows:—

To two cups small whole vegetables, or two cups of vegetables mashed or sliced, add a rounding teaspoonful of butter, and half a level teaspoonful of salt. To beans, peas, and squash, add one-half teaspoonful of sugar to improve them. Add milk or the vegetable liquid when additional moisture is required.

POTATOES

Pre-eminent among vegetables stands the potato. The solid matter of potatoes consists largely of starch, with a small quantity of albumen and mineral salts. Potatoes also contain an acid juice, the greater portion of which lies near the skin. This bitter principle is set free by heat. While potatoes are being boiled, it passes into the water; in baking it escapes with the steam.

New potatoes may be compared to unripe fruit, as the starch grains are not fully matured. Potatoes are at their best in the fall, and they keep well during the winter. In the spring, when germination commences, the starch changes to dextrin or gum, rendering the potato more waxy when cooked, and the sugar then formed makes them sweeter. When the potatoes are frozen, the same change takes place.

In the spring, when potatoes are shriveled and gummy, soaking improves them, as the water thus absorbed dissolves the gum, and makes them less sticky. At other times, long soaking is undesirable.

Soak about half an hour in the fall, one to three hours in winter and spring. Never serve potatoes, whether boiled or baked, in a closely covered dish, as they thus become sodden and clammy; but cover with a folded napkin, and allow the moisture to escape. They require about forty-five minutes to one hour to bake, if of a good size, and should be served promptly when done.

BAKED POTATOES

Potatoes are either baked in their jackets or peeled; in either case they should not be exposed to a fierce heat, inasmuch as thereby a great deal of the vegetable is scorched and rendered uneatable. They should be frequently turned while being baked, and kept from touching one another in the oven or dish. When they are pared, they should be baked in a dish, and oil of some kind added, to prevent their outsides from becoming burned.

MASHED POTATOES

Pare and boil or steam six or eight large potatoes. If boiled, drain when tender, and let set in the kettle for a few minutes, keeping them covered, shaking the kettle occasionally to prevent scorching. Mash with a wire potato masher, or, if convenient, press through a colander; add salt, a lump of butter, and sufficient hot milk to moisten thoroughly. Whip with the batter whip, or wooden spoon, until light and fluffy. Heap up on a plate, press a lump of butter into the top, and send to the table hot.

POTATO PUFFS

Potatoes, prepared as for mashed potatoes, 2 cups.
Cream or milk, ¾ cup.
Melted butter, 2 tablespoonfuls.
Eggs, yolks and whites beaten separately, 2.
Salt.
Mix and beat up thoroughly, folding in the beaten whites last. Make into balls, put into greased pans, brush with beaten egg, and bake a light brown.

MINCED POTATOES

Mince six large, cold potatoes. Put them in a baking-pan, cover with milk; add a little cream, and bake fifteen minutes.

SCALLOPED POTATOES NO. 1

Potatoes, medium size, 6.
Milk sufficient to cover, mixed
   with tablespoonful of flour.
Crumbs.
Butter.
Salt.

Cut potatoes into even slices, put in a baking-pan, sprinkle with a little salt, and a few small pieces of butter. Pour over the milk and flour mixture, and sprinkle the top with a layer of crumbs. Cover and bake till potatoes are tender. Remove the cover and brown lightly .

SCALLOPED POTATOES NO. 2

Cold, boiled potatoes, sliced.
Thin cream sauce.

Place in alternate layers in a pan and sprinkle the top with ground bread crumbs. Bake until brown.

HASHED BROWNED POTATOES

Use cold, boiled potatoes or good left-over baked potatoes. Pare and cut into three-quarter-inch dice or irregular pieces. Put in a shallow baking-pan, sprinkle with salt, pour over sufficient cooking oil, season well, and prevent scorching. Put into the oven, and when they begin to brown, stir continually till all are nicely browned.

NEW POTATOES AND CREAM

New potatoes.
Cream.
Salt.
Butter.
Parsley.

Wash and rub new potatoes with a coarse cloth or scrubbing brush; drop into boiling water and boil briskly till done, but no more. Press the potato against the side of the kettle with a fork; if done, it will yield to gentle pressure. In a saucepan have ready some butter and cream, hot but not boiling, a little green parsley, and salt. Drain the potatoes, add the mixture, put over hot water a minute or two, and serve.

POTATOES A LA CREME

Cold, boiled potatoes, 2 cups.
Parsley, finely chopped.
Flour.
Milk.
Butter, 1 tablespoonful.
Salt.

Heat the milk and stir in the butter cut up in the flour. Stir until smooth and thick. Salt and add the potatoes, sliced, and a very little finely-chopped parsley. Shake over the fire until the potatoes are heated through. Pour into a deep dish and serve.

POTATOES A LA DELMONICO

Cut the potatoes with a vegetable cutter into small balls about the size of marbles. Put them into stew-pan with plenty of butter and a good sprinkling of salt. Keep the saucepan covered and shake occasionally until they are quite done, which will be in about an hour.

POTATO CROQUETTES (DELMONICO'S)

Cold, mashed potatoes, 2 cups.
Flour or cracker crumbs.
Salt.
Eggs, 2.
Butter.
Cooking oil.

Season the potatoes with salt and butter. Beat the whites of the eggs and work all together thoroughly. Make into small balls slightly flattened. Dip them into beaten yolks of eggs, roll in flour or cracker crumbs, and fry in hot oil.

STEWED SALSIFY OR VEGETABLE OYSTERS

Salsify, cut in ¼-inch slices, 1 quart.
Milk, 2 cups.
Butter, 1 tablespoonful.
Salt to taste.

Wash and scrape the salsify, slice, and put into cold water to prevent discoloring. Cook in sufficient boiling water to cover. When tender, drain, add the milk and butter, let simmer a few minutes, and serve.

ESCALLOPED VEGETABLE OYSTER

Sliced vegetable oyster, 3 cups.
Rich cream sauce.
Sifted bread crumbs.
Salt.

Wash, scrape, cut in thin slices, and put into plenty of cold water till ready to use, to prevent discoloration. When ready to cook, boil in enough water to prevent scorching. Salt when they begin to get tender. Boil a few minutes longer, but do not let them get too salt. Drain, or remove with a skimmer, putting a layer in a baking-pan, then a little rich cream sauce, then another layer of each. Sprinkle the top with sifted bread crumbs, and bake a light brown.

MOCK OYSTERS

Corn, young and tender, 6 ears.
Flour, 3 tablespoonfuls.
Butter, 3 tablespoonfuls.
Eggs, 3.
Oil.
Salt, 3 teaspoonfuls.

Grate the corn with a coarse grater into a deep dish; beat the whites and yolks separately, and add the corn, flour, butter, and salt. Drop spoonfuls of this batter into a frying-pan with hot oil, and fry a light brown on both sides. The corn must be young.

CELERY

Cut off all the roots and remove all the decayed and outside leaves. Wash thoroughly, being careful to remove all specks and blemishes. If the stalks are large, divide them lengthwise into two or three pieces and place root downward in a celery glass, which should be nearly filled with cold water.

STEWED CELERY

Celery hearts, 6.
White sauce, 2 cups.

Cut the celery into half-inch lengths and cook in boiling, salted water. When tender, drain and pour over this the sauce. Heat well, and serve. The liquid drained from the celery may be thickened, seasoned with a little butter, and used instead of the white sauce if preferred.

LENTILS (ORIENTAL STYLE)

Lentils, 1 cup.
Olive oil, 2 tablespoonfuls.
Salt, 1 level teaspoonful.
Boiled rice, 1 cup.
Onion, finely shredded, 1.

Wash the lentils well, soak overnight, and drain. Cook in boiling water till tender; drain again. Put the olive oil in a saucepan, add the onion, and cook till the onion is soft, not brown. Add the lentils and boiled rice, mix, stir over the fire till hot, add the salt. and serve hot.

LENTILS WITH ONIONS

Lentils, 1 cup.
Onions, 2.
Butter.

Wash the lentils, put to cook in saucepan with plenty of cold water, and boil till tender; when soft, turn them into a fine colander, and drain thoroughly, saving the water they were cooked in. Peel the onions, cut into thin slices, put in a flat stew-pan with a lump of butter, or a little olive oil, and fry. Put the lentils in the onions and add salt to taste. Moisten with a little of the broth drained from the lentils and allow them to simmer at the side of the fire. Serve.

CREAMED CHESTNUTS

Boil or steam the chestnuts till tender. Make a cream sauce of milk or cream, seasoned with butter, and slightly thickened with flour. Pour this over the chestnuts; serve as a vegetable.

ASPARAGUS NO. 1

Asparagus, like potatoes, contains a bitter alkaloid, which is drawn into the water in cooking, and often imparts to it a very unpleasant flavor. This may be remedied by blanching the asparagus in boiling water for four or five minutes. Then drain, and add more hot water, and finish cooking.

ASPARAGUS NO. 2

Scrape the stalk ends of the asparagus or break off the tough lower stalks as far as they will snap.

Wash well, tie in bundles, and put into enough rapidly-boiling salted water to cover. Allow a teaspoonful of salt to each quart of water; cook uncovered from twenty to thirty minutes, or till perfectly tender. Drain, remove the string, spread with salt and butter, and serve immediately on toast. The asparagus may be neatly arranged on hot toast and covered with white cream sauce, if preferred.

ASPARAGUS POMPADOUR

Wash the asparagus carefully, place in a saucepan of boiling salted water, and boil till done. Take them out and cut into lengths of about two inches, and place on a cloth near the fire to dry. Prepare a little sauce made of lemon juice, butter, yolk of an egg, and salt. Place the asparagus on a dish, over which pour the sauce, and serve.

PEAS

The flavor of peas and the time required for cooking depend largely upon their freshness. Very young peas will cook tender in twenty minutes, older peas sometimes requiring an hour or more. A teaspoonful of finely minced parsley cooked with peas imparts to them a very delicious flavor.

STEWED ASPARAGUS

Break the tender parts of the asparagus into one-inch lengths and put into enough boiling water to cover. Boil till tender; add sufficient rich milk or cream to make a gravy. Thicken with flour, season with salt, let come to a boil, and serve.

ASPARAGUS WITH EGGS

Asparagus.
Cream, 2 tablespoonfuls.
Salt.
Eggs, 4.
Butter, 1 tablespoonful.

Cut the tender tops from a bunch of asparagus, and boil about twenty minutes. Then put into a baking-tin with butter and salt. Beat the whites and yolks of the eggs separately, add the cream and pour this over the asparagus. Bake until the eggs are set.

ASPARAGUS WITH GREEN PEAS

Asparagus, 2 cups.
Peas, 2 cups.
Salt.
Rich milk or cream.
Flour.

Break the tender parts of the asparagus into one-inch lengths and put with the peas into boiling water enough to cover. Boil till tender; add sufficient rich milk or cream to make a gravy. Thicken with flour, season with salt, let come to a boil, and serve.

BAKED BEANS

Wash one and three-fourths cups of navy beans and put them into an earthen jar, covering immedi-

9

ately with one and three-fourths quarts of boiling
water. Add salt, cover, and put into the oven.
When they boil well, draw the jar to the edge of
the oven, where they will just simmer. Cook for
twenty-four hours. If they get too dry, add a little
boiling water. The beans will be nicely colored and
have a rich flavor.

BAKED BEANS

Small white beans, 2 cups.
Protose, if desired.
Molasses, 1 teaspoonful.
Salt.

Clean the beans, soak in cold water one hour,
season with salt and molasses. Put into a covered
jar with plenty of water; bake overnight in a slow
oven. When done, the beans should be whole, dry,
and mealy, and of a rich brown color. This can
only be obtained by baking the beans several hours
in a slow oven. If desired, a little chopped protose
may be added. Serve the beans plain, or with brown
bread.

PUREE OF BEANS

Follow the directions given for puree of peas.

BEANS STEWED

Wash the required quantity of navy, lima, kidney,
or other beans, and put to cook in plenty of boiling

water; boil till they are swollen, then put them where they will stew till cooked; season just before they finish cooking. Never parboil beans.

BAKED BEANS WITH TOMATO SAUCE

Prepare the beans as for plain baked beans; put into the jars to bake; cover with a mixture of strained stewed tomatoes and water in equal proportions; a little butter or olive oil may be added.

SUCCOTASH

Fresh shelled lima beans, 2 cups.
Sweet corn, 2 ears.
Cream, ½ cup.
Butter, size of an egg.
Salt.

Put beans in pot with cold water, rather more than will cover them. Scrape the kernels from twelve ears of young sweet corn. Put the cobs in with the peas, boiling from thirty to forty-five minutes. Take out the cobs and put in the scraped corn. Boil again for fifteen minutes; then season with salt, butter and cream. Serve hot.

ONIONS

Contrary to the opinion of many, the onion is not objectionable as an article of food. Judiciously used it fills as important a place in cooking as salt or any other seasoning.

BAKED ONIONS

Onions, large, 6.
Salt.
Crumbs.
Milk.
Butter.

Put onions into a saucepan of water, or water and milk mixed in equal proportions; add salt and boil till tender. When done so that they can be easily mashed, work them up with a little butter into a paste. Cover with bread crumbs and bake in a moderate oven.

STUFFED ONIONS

Peel the desired number of onions, being careful not to cut off the root end. Take out the inside of the onion and fill the hole with a mixture of bread crumbs, beaten egg, and a little milk. Season with salt and sage. Bake in oven until brown.

SCRAMBLED TOMATOES

Tomatoes, 6.
Eggs, 3.
Butter.
Salt.

Remove the skins from six tomatoes and cut them up in a saucepan. Add a little butter and salt. When sufficiently boiled beat up eggs, and just before you serve turn them into the saucepan with the tomatoes, and stir one way for two minutes, allowing them time to get thoroughly done.

SPINACH

Trim the spinach and wash in three or four waters to remove the grit. Cook in boiling water about twenty minutes, removing the scum. Do not cover the vessel while cooking. When tender, turn into a colander, drain, and press well. Chop fine, put into a saucepan with butter and salt. Set on the fire and cook till quite dry, stirring it all the time. Turn into a vegetable dish, shape, and garnish with slices of hard-boiled eggs.

SUMMER SQUASH

Wash and cut in pieces. Cook in the steamer, that it may be as dry as possible. When done, let it stand and drain a few minutes, shaking it occasionally. Mash and season with salt, butter, and a little cream.

WINTER SQUASH (HUBBARD)

Mashed:

Cut the squash, pare, remove seeds, wash, and put into the steamer. Cook until soft, remove and mash or press through a colander. Season with salt, butter, sugar, and a little sweet cream. Beat well, and serve.

Baked:

Cut into pieces of desired size, remove seeds, sprinkle with a little sugar and salt; bake until done. Serve in the shell, or it may be peeled before baking.

PUREE OF PEAS

Peas, fresh, 2 cups (or dry, 1 cup).
Butter, 1 tablespoonful.
Cream or milk, 1½ cups.
Flour, 1 level tablespoonful.
Salt, 1 teaspoonful.

Put the peas to cook in boiling water; boil until tender, then simmer slowly, cooking as dry as possible without scorching. When soft and dry, rub through a colander to remove the hulls. Put the butter in a saucepan; when melted stir in the flour, being careful not to scorch; pour in the milk gradually, stirring all the time; and when thoroughly cooked, add the salt and the pulp of the peas. Turn all into a double boiler, heat thoroughly, and serve.

GREEN CORN (STEWED)

Green corn, 3 cups.
Butter.
Salt.
Milk, more or less, 1 cup.
Sugar.

Husk and clean as for boiling corn; with a sharp knife cut off the top of the grain, being careful not to cut too close to the cob and with the back of the knife press out the remaining pulp. When cut in this way, the corn is much more juicy than when the grains are cut close to the cob. Place the milk in a granite saucepan, and when boiling, add the butter and corn; cook from ten to fifteen minutes, or until

it loses its raw taste. Stir frequently, and season
to taste with salt and sugar.

GREEN CORN (BOILED)

Strip off the husk, remove the silk, put into fresh
boiling water, and cook ten to twenty minutes.
Cook only till done, for if boiled too long, the corn
hardens, and its flavor is impaired. If the corn is
not very sweet, add one-fourth cup of sugar to the
water in which it is boiled.

GREEN PEAS (VERY YOUNG AND TENDER)

Shell the peas and cover with cold water; skim off
undeveloped peas which rise to the top of the water
and drain. Barely cover with boiling water; cook
till tender, then add salt. When done, very little
water should remain. Season to taste with butter
and add more salt if needed. A little sugar is sometimes an improvement.

When the peas are older, half a cup of milk or
cream, with sufficient flour to thicken, is considered
an improvement.

PLAIN BOILED STRING BEANS

Break off the ends of beans and string; wash
thoroughly; if large cut them in two; drop into
boiling water and boil till tender. Salt and season
with olive oil or butter; if preferred, drain off the
juice, salt to taste, and add some hot, rich milk.

CAULIFLOWER WITH CREAM SAUCE

Divide the cauliflower into portions of convenient size before cooking. Boil slowly, or steam till tender, drain, and when dished up, pour one or two tablespoonfuls of strained white sauce over each portion.

BAKED CAULIFLOWER
Cauliflower.
Milk, 1 cup.
Flour, 1 rounded teaspoonful.
Butter, 1 rounded teaspoonful.
Salt.

Soak a medium head of cauliflower in cold water with head down for thirty minutes; steam or boil gently till tender; separate into small sprays and pour over them a sauce made of the milk thickened with flour and butter beaten together. Add a little salt. Cover lightly with bread crumbs, which have been moistened with melted butter, and bake until a nice brown. Serve at once.

CAULIFLOWER WITH TOMATO SAUCE

Prepare as for stewed cauliflower, and when done serve with tomato sauce.
Sauce:

Strain a pint of stewed tomatoes, let come to a boil, and thicken with a tablespoonful of flour rubbed smooth in a little water; add a little olive oil or hot cream; salt to taste. Pour this over the cauliflower, and serve.

STEWED CAULIFLOWER

Prepare as for plain boiled cauliflower; cook or steam till tender; drain and put in a stew-pan; pour over some rich milk or cream; stew together for a few minutes, and serve.

BOILED CAULIFLOWER (PLAIN)

Pick off the outside leaves, cut the stalk one inch from the head, split, wash thoroughly in cold water. Put in saited water for one or two hours before cooking. Cook in salted, boiling water (milk added to the water will keep it white). Boil till tender; remove from the fire; let stand in same water till ready to serve. Drain, serve with cream, butter, or egg sauce poured over.

BROWNED CAULIFLOWER

Prepare as for plain boiled cauliflower; boil until tender; place in a baking-dish and sprinkle with fine bread crumbs; pour over some thin cream sauce, and brown in the oven. Serve with egg or butter sauce.

CABBAGE AND CREAM

Cabbage, 1 head.
Grated nutmeg.
Cream, 1½ cups.
Butter, 2 tablespoonfuls.
Flour, 1 teaspoonful.
Salt.

Take a well-blanched cabbage, drain, cool, and chop fine; place it in a stew-pan with butter, a little salt, and grated nutmeg; add the flour, stirring well, and then pour in the cream. Stir till the cabbage and cream are thoroughly mixed. Cook about thirty or forty minutes, and serve hot.

BAKED CABBAGE NO. 1

Wash and chop rather fine the required quantity of cabbage. Put into a stew-pan with boiling water; add a little salt and blanch twenty minutes. Drain, put in a baking-pan, and cover with cream or milk to which has been added the beaten yolk of one egg to each cup of cream. Bake until the custard is nicely set.

BAKED CABBAGE NO. 2

Cabbage, cold, boiled.
Browned crumbs.
Butter.
Salt.
Egg, well beaten, 1.
Brown sauce.
Nutmeg.

Rub sufficient cold, boiled cabbage through a sieve or colander. Mix with it a piece of butter, salt, nutmeg, and the well-beaten egg. Stir thoroughly; butter a pudding dish of suitable size, line with browned crumbs, press in the cabbage, and bake in a moderate oven. Turn out on a hot dish, pour brown sauce around the base, and serve.

CABBAGE STEWED WITH TOMATO

Slice and wash a good sound cabbage and put into a stew-pan with enough chopped tomato to give it a decidedly tart taste. Add enough salt to season. Add sufficient water to cook and stew slowly till tender. Strained tomatoes may be used if desired.

SCALLOPED CABBAGE

Wash and chop the cabbage in rather fine pieces. Put a layer of the cabbage into a baking-pan and sprinkle with a little salt. Cover this with finely-broken, fresh bread crumbs, repeat and pour over sufficient milk or cream to thoroughly moisten and cover the crumbs. Cover and bake in a moderate oven till the cabbage is thoroughly cooked. More milk may be added if necessary.

HOLLAND CREAM CABBAGE

Cabbage.
Eggs, 2.
Water, 2 cups.
Lemon juice, 2 tablespoonfuls.
Salt.
Butter.

Cut the cabbage fine, sprinkle with salt, and let stand a few minutes before using. Beat the eggs well, add lemon juice, water, and melted butter. Mix this with the cabbage and cook till tender in a vessel that does not easily burn.

HOT SLAW

Clean a nice young head of cabbage, quarter, cut out the heart, and shred fine. Put in cold, salted water for half an hour; drain, boil till tender; drain partly, leaving enough juice to make the cabbage moist; add lemon juice and a little butter or olive oil; season with salt; serve hot.

LADIES' CABBAGE

Firm, white cabbage, 1.
Butter, 1 tablespoonful.
Salt.
Eggs, 2.
Cream, rich, 1 tablespoonful.

Boil a firm, white cabbage fifteen minutes, changing the water; add more from the boiling teakettle; when tender, drain, and set aside till perfectly cold; chop fine and add the beaten eggs, butter, salt, and cream; stir all well together and bake in a buttered dish till brown.

BRUSSELS SPROUTS PLAIN

Select nice, fresh sprouts, cut off the stem end and outside leaves, and wash in cold water. Cook in salted water till tender. Pour off the water; serve with butter or cream sauce.

BRUSSELS SPROUTS SAUTE

Prepare as for plain boiled; when done, drain and press dry; put in a stew-pan, season with salt,

and moisten with oil and rich milk. Toss frequently and cook till well heated through. Serve
hot with mashed potato.

BRUSSELS SPROUTS BAKED WITH
CRUMBS

Prepare as for plain boiled; when done, drain,
and press dry; arrange in a baking-dish and sprinkle
with bread crumbs; pour over a thin cream or egg
sauce. Bake in the oven till nicely browned.

BEETS

Select young red beets; cut off the tops half an
inch from the root. If cut too close, the roots will
bleed and the color will be impaired. Wash and
clean carefully with the brush to remove all particles
of dirt. They may be boiled or steamed. If boiled,
use as little water as possible. Young beets will
cook in an hour; old beets require three or four
hours, according to age and size. When done, put
in cold water, rub off the skins, and they are ready
for use.

BEET GREENS

Wash young, tender beet tops, cleaning thoroughly; drain and boil in salted water till tender;
drain, chop fine, season with butter or oil, and
serve with lemon juice or cream.

BEET STALKS WITH BUTTER SAUCE

Take some beet stalks, cut off the leaves, wash
thoroughly, tie in bunches, and let steep in cold water

two or three hours to make them fresh and crisp.
Boil in salted water until tender; cut the band;
serve as asparagus on a platter with butter sauce.

BEETS AND POTATOES

Boil young beets and new potatoes separately
until tender; peel and slice in alternate layers in a
baking dish; season with salt and moisten with rich
milk. Bake until nicely browned.

BAKED BEETS

Select young, smooth, red beets of uniform size;
wash and clean thoroughly; bake in a slow oven
from two to six hours; when done, remove the skins
and dress with lemon juice or cream sauce.

BOILED BEETS

Cut off the tops half an inch from the roots; wash
and clean carefully to remove all dirt. Boil in as
little water as possible. When done, pour a little
cold water over them, rub off the skins, and slice
into a granite or earthen dish; pour over them equal
parts of lemon juice and water. Let stand one or
two hours before serving.

YOUNG BEETS

Cream or milk, 1 cup.
Flour, 1 tablespoonful.
Butter, 1 tablespoonful.
Beets.

Cook the beets till tender in salted water, then cut into dice. Serve with cream sauce, made by thickening the milk or cream with the flour rubbed in the butter. Heat well, and serve at once.

BEET AND POTATO HASH

Cold, boiled beets, 2 cups.
Cold, boiled potatoes, 2 cups.
Salt.
Butter.
Cream.

Chop beets and potatoes fine and season with salt and butter. Pour over a little cream. Put on the stove in a covered saucepan, and stir occasionally. When thoroughly heated through, serve.

BAKED PARSNIPS

Scrape and cut in half lengthwise; boil till tender; put in a shallow baking-pan; put a few pieces of chopped butter or a little cooking oil on top; sprinkle lightly with sugar; pour over sufficient cream to about half cover. Salt to taste and bake a rich brown.

PARSNIPS IN EGG SAUCE

Clean and cut into small dice and boil in a little salted water until tender, drain and pour over sufficient egg sauce to cover.

STEWED PARSNIPS

After washing the parsnips, slice them about half an inch thick; put them in a saucepan containing enough boiling water to barely cook them; add a tablespoonful of butter, season with salt, then cover closely and stew them until the water has cooked away, stirring often to prevent burning, until they are soft. When they are done, they will be of a creamy, light straw color, and deliciously sweet, retaining all the nutrition of the vegetable.

YOUNG TURNIPS

Cut into half-inch dice and boil till tender; drain and add a small lump of butter and a little salt; heat well and add a dash of lemon juice at the last.

MASHED TURNIPS

Turnips may be cooked and mashed the same as potatoes, keeping them as dry as possible. The addition of a little sugar is considered an improvement by some.

HOLLAND BOILED TURNIP

Turnips, cut in ¾-inch dice, 1 quart.
Egg, 1.
Butter, ½ cup.
Lemon, large, 1.

Boil the turnips till tender in just enough salted water to prevent burning; drain and set in a covered dish on the side of the range, where they will keep hot but not burn. Melt the butter, add the beaten yolk with the eggs, juice of the lemon, and a little salt. Serve a spoonful of this sauce over each order of turnip.

FRENCH CARROTS

Scrape enough small round carrots to make three cups; boil in salted water till tender; drain, and cover with a rich parsley sauce.

CARROTS A LA CREME

Clean carrots, cut in slices about half an inch thick, and parboil in salted water. Drain, pour over some hot rich milk, and let simmer till done. Add a little butter; season with salt.

CARROTS WITH EGG SAUCE

Clean carrots, cut in slices about half an inch thick, and boil until tender; drain, pour egg sauce over, and serve.

PUREE OF CARROTS

Clean young carrots, cut into slices, and boil in salted water until tender. Drain, mash through a colander, and season with a little salt and cream. Serve as mashed potatoes, or with broiled or braized protose as an entree.

10

TO DRESS CUCUMBERS

Pare and lay in cold water—ice water if possible—
for an hour. Slice very thin. Sprinkle a very little
fine salt over each piece. Let stand for an hour.
Shake the dish briskly, drain closely, sprinkle with
lemon juice, and serve.

SAUCES
For Vegetables, Entrees, Puddings, Etc

VEGETABLE SOUP STOCK NO. 1

Cooking oil, ½ cup.
Butter, ¼ cup.

Put into a saucepan and add
Carrot, medium, 1.
Turnip, 1.
Celery stalks, with root, 2.
Parsley sprigs, 2 or 3.
Onions, large, 2.
Bay leaves, 2.

All to be chopped fine; place on range and cook slowly, stirring occasionally to prevent burning, until vegetables are nicely browned, then add

Flour, ½ cup.

Stir and mix thoroughly, until a rich brown, being careful not to burn. Now add

Strained tomato, 1 cup.
Boiling water to required consistency.

Strain through a fine sieve, and the stock is ready for use.

VEGETABLE STOCK NO. 2

Boil some turnips, carrots, celery, and onions in enough water to make half the amount of stock required. When the vegetables are done, drain and add an equal amount of rich bean broth with a little brown flour, nut butter, celery salt, and just enough

strained tomato to remove the sweet vegetable
taste. This should be of the consistency of broth
when done. Use with roast braized protose, etc.
Protose may be cooked with the vegetables if it can
be afforded. The vegetables should be put to cook
in cold water that the substance and flavor may be
well drawn out.

OLIVE SAUCE

Take one-fourth cup of ripe olives, and after ex-
tracting the stones, chop fine. Put on the stove
and stew for two or three hours in water enough
to cover well. Brown together a little olive oil
and flour, the same as for gravy. Strain through a
colander and add the stewed olives. Season with
salt.

BROWN REGENCY SAUCE

(For Vegetables and Roasts)

Nut butter, 1 cup.
Sage, 1 tablespoonful.
Browned flour, 3 heaping tablespoonfuls.
Salt.
Minced onion, 2 tablespoonfuls.
Water 1½ quarts.

Mix all together, salt lightly, put in an enameled
baking-pan, cover, and bake till of the desired consistency.

HOLLANDAISE SAUCE

Butter, 1 tablespoonful.
Olive oil, 1 tablespoonful.
Flour, 1 tablespoonful.
Salt.
Lemon juice, 2 tablespoonfuls.
Eggs, 2.
Nutmeg.

Rub the butter, flour, nutmeg, and salt together until smooth, and add slowly one and one-half cups hot water, stirring constantly. Boil, remove from the fire, and add the lemon juice, olive oil, and the yolks of the eggs, one at a time. Beat slowly and thoroughly together. Strain, and serve.

SAUCE IMPERIAL

Stewed tomatoes, 1 quart.
Bay leaves, 2.
Onion, medium, 1.
Lemon, ¼.
Chopped parsley, 1 tablespoonful.
Thyme, 1 teaspoonful.
Cooking oil, 2 tablespoonfuls.
Flour, 2 tablespoonfuls.

Put the oil, parsley, bay leaves, thyme, and onions into a stew-pan, set on the range and cook until the onion is a golden brown, being careful not to burn; then add the flour, let cook a few minutes, add the lemon and tomato, and let stew half an hour. Strain, salt, and serve. The chopped parsley may be added just before serving, if desired.

MINT SAUCE

Mint, ¼ cup.
Sugar, ⅓ cup.
Lemon juice, ½ cup.

Mix all together, set on the side of the range where the sugar will melt, and the sauce be hot, but it must not get too hot.   Serve with protose or meat substitutes.

WHITE CREAM SAUCE FOR VEGETABLES

Butter, 2 rounding tablespoonfuls.
Flour, 2 rounding tablespoonfuls.
Milk, 2 cups.
Salt, ½ teaspoonful.

Melt the butter in a saucepan, add the flour, and cook until well blended, but not browned; add the milk gradually, and stir until boiling well; then add the salt.

Half milk and half broth of the vegetables may be used if desired, unless the broth has a bitter or otherwise objectionable taste, as is sometimes the case with asparagus.

GERMAN SAUCE

Egg yolks, 12.
Fruit juice, bright colored, 1 cup.
Sugar, ½ cup.
Juice of ½ lemon.

Beat the yolks of the eggs about two minutes; put the sugar into a saucepan with the fruit juice (preferably cherry or strawberry); stir it over the fire till hot, then remove it to the side, as it must not be permitted to boil. Stir in the beaten yolks and add the lemon juice. Whisk the sauce at the side of the fire until well frothed and thickened.

TOMATO SAUCE

Tomatoes, stewed, 1 quart.
Butter, 1 tablespoonful.
Salt.
Minced onion, 1 tablespoonful.
Flour, 1 tablespoonful.

Put the tomatoes into a saucepan over the fire; add the onion and salt; boil about twenty minutes; remove from range and strain through a sieve. In another pan melt the butter, and as it melts sprinkle in the flour; stir till it browns and froths a little. Mix the tomato pulp with it, and it is ready for use.

IDEAL CHILI SAUCE

Stewed tomatoes, 1 quart.
Celery salt, 1 teaspoonful.
Sugar, 1 tablespoonful.
Sliced onion, large, 1.
Salt, 1½ teaspoonfuls.

Mix all together and let simmer two or three hours. Strain through a sieve. Serve with croquettes, broiled protose, or nuttolene.

NUT GRAVY NO. 1

Nut butter, 4 tablespoonfuls.
Strained tomatoes, 1 cup.
Hot water, 2 cups.

Thoroughly mix the butter with the water and tomato. Let it boil, and salt to taste. If too thin, thicken with a little flour rubbed smooth in a little water.

NUT GRAVY NO. 2

Water, 1 quart.
Strained tomatoes, 1½ cups.
Salt to taste.
Nut butter, 1 heaped tablespoonful.
Flour.

Emulsify the butter in the tomato, add to the water, and put in a saucepan over the fire, being careful not to scorch. When it boils, thicken with a little flour rubbed smooth in water, using plenty of salt to season, as it brings out the nice flavor of the sauce.

CREAM TOMATO SAUCE

Make a tomato sauce and add one-fourth part rich cream, beating well.

TOMATO CREAM SAUCE

Make a rich cream sauce and add one-fourth part of strained tomatoes, or an equal amount of tomato sauce. Beat up well.

BROWN SAUCE FOR VEGETABLES AND ROASTS

Water 2 cups.
Minced onion, small, 1.
Browned flour, 2 rounded tablespoonfuls.
Strained tomato enough to mix the flour smooth
Salt.
Minced protose, ¼ cup.
Butter, 1 rounded tablespoonful.
White flour, 1 tablespoonful.
Celery salt.

Put the water, butter, and onion in a saucepan and set on the stove; when it begins to boil, add the protose and let simmer ten or fifteen minutes, then place where it will boil, and thicken with the browned and white flour rubbed smooth in the tomato; the thickening should be thin enough to pour readily. Let cook a few minutes and add salt and celery salt, and serve with vegetables or roasts.

WALNUT GRAVY

Ground walnuts, 1 cup.
Milk, 1 cup.
Flour.
Water, 2 cups.
Salt to taste.

Put the water and milk in a saucepan, and when boiling add the walnuts. Thicken with a little flour thickening, and salt to taste.

PARSLEY SAUCE

Add two tablespoonfuls of finely chopped parsley to two cups of cream sauce.

BROWN SAUCE

Vegetable stock, 2 cups.
Browned flour, 2 tablespoonfuls.
Strained tomatoes, ¼ cup.

Heat the stock to boiling, add the hot tomato, and thicken with browned flour.

CREAM SAUCE

Cream, ½ cup.
Flour, 1 heaped tablespoonful.
Milk, 2½ cups.

Mix the flour to a smooth cream in a little milk, boil the cream and remainder of the milk, and thicken with the flour. Salt to taste. If a richer sauce is desired, the beaten yolks of one or two eggs may be added.

EGG SAUCE

Cream sauce, 1 pint.
Egg, 1.

Beat the egg and add to the cream sauce, mixing thoroughly.

BREAD SAUCE

Stale bread crumbs, 1 cup.
Chopped onion, 1.
Butter, 1 large teaspoonful.
Vegetable stock, 1 cup.
Mace, ¼ teaspoonful.

Rub the bread crumbs through a sieve and add the onion and mace. Boil for a few minutes in the vegetable stock, add the butter, and serve.

HARD SAUCE

Butter, ¾ pound.
Powdered sugar, 1 pound.
Nutmeg to suit.

Beat the butter and sugar together until white and creamy, then add the nutmeg.

GOLDEN SAUCE

Nutmeg, ½
Sugar, 1 cup.
Butter, 1 rounding tablespoonful.
Egg yolks, 2.
Corn starch, 1 tablespoonful.
Water, 2 cups.

Break the nutmeg into pieces and put in a saucepan with the water, boil, and add the corn starch mixed (sifted) with the sugar. Stir over the fire until the corn starch is cooked, then add the butter. Beat the yolks with one tablespoonful of the sauce, then stir quickly into the remainder, which should be immediately removed. as the yolks will curdle if boiled. Strain, and serve.

VANILLA SAUCE

> Cream, 2 cups.
> Eggs, 3.
> Flour, 2 tablespoonfuls.
> Sugar and vanilla to taste.

Thicken the cream with the flour and stir in the beaten yolks. Cook a few minutes, stirring all the time. Add sugar to taste. When cool, add the beaten whites, and flavor with vanilla.

ORANGE SAUCE

> Oranges, 2.
> Eggs, 2.
> Butter to suit.
> Sugar, 1 cup.
> Lemon juice, ¼ cup.

Put the juice of the oranges and the grated rind of one with the sugar into a saucepan. Set on the range and stir till the sugar is melted or dissolved, then strain through a fine sieve to remove the rind. Add the beaten eggs, lemon juice, and butter. Before serving, set in double boiler and stir for a few minutes to melt the butter and thoroughly mix the eggs. Serve hot or cold.

LEMON SAUCE FOR PUDDING NO. 1

Sugar, 2 cups.
Eggs, 2.
Lemons, 2.
Boiling water, 1½ cups.

Add the grated rind and juice of the lemons to
the sugar, beat the eggs until light, and add to the
sugar, and stir well. Just before serving, add the
boiling water and set on the stove, but do not boil.
For a richer sauce add one-third of a cup of butter.

LEMON SAUCE NO. 2

Water, 2 cups.
Corn starch, 3 tablespoonfuls.
Butter, 1 tablespoonful.
Sugar, 1 cup.
Lemon, grated rind and juice, 1.

Boil the sugar in the water for five minutes, then
stir in the corn starch previously mixed with a little
cold water. Stir over the fire ten minutes, then add
the grated rind and juice of the lemon and the butter.
When the butter is melted, the sauce is ready for
use.

SAUCE FOR PLUM PUDDING

Butter, 1 large tablespoonful.
Hot water, 1½ cups.
Lemon juice, 1 tablespoonful.
Flour, 2 tablespoonfuls.
Brown sugar, 1 cup.
Grated nutmeg.

Put the butter into a saucepan; when it has melted stir in the flour and mix well; then pour in gradually the hot water and stir over the fire till well cooked; then add the sugar, lemon juice and a small quantity of grated nutmeg.

EGGS

OMELETS

Omelets may be made with asparagus, cauliflower, lima beans, onions, peas, lentils, granose, gluten, rice, nuts, etc.

Boil the vegetables till tender, chop fine, then beat with the eggs and proceed as with plain omelets.

OMELET SOUFFLE NO. 1

Take two eggs, separate whites from yolks, beat whites very stiff, salt, and add yolks, beating just enough to mix yolks with whites. Turn into a hot oiled omelet pan, put in medium hot oven, and bake till done, or to a rich brown. Serve in great haste on being removed from the oven, to prevent falling.

OMELET SOUFFLE NO. 2

Eggs, 4.
Powdered sugar, 2 tablespoonfuls.
Flavoring.

Beat the yolks of the eggs as light as possible, and add the sugar, a few drops of flavoring, and beat to a cream. Beat the whites until you can turn the plate bottom side up, without their falling. Pour the beaten whites and yolks together and mix thoroughly. Put into an oiled baking dish, and dust with powdered sugar. Bake in a moderate oven till a golden brown. Serve at once.

A very delicate souffle is made of whites of eggs beaten stiff, adding a tablespoonful of sugar to two whites, and chopped apricots or peaches. Any kind of marmalade may be used in place of fruit.

PLAIN OMELET (FRENCH)

Break eggs into a dish, whip lightly with egg whip or fork, turn into hot oiled skillet, and place on range. As soon as they begin to set, lift edges of omelet, so that the uncoagulated part can run under, next to bottom of the skillet. When light brown, turn, and cook till light brown on the other side. Fold with knife about one-third over; then toss out on hot platter, so that the one-third fold will be underneath. Garnish with parsley and water-cress. Serve at once.

PROTOSE OMELET

Protose, ½ a thin slice.
Eggs, 2.
Minced parsley.
Cooking oil.

Mince the protose fine, break two eggs, separating the whites, beat the yolks a little, and stir the minced protose into them. Beat the whites into a froth, not stiff, and stir into the protose; add a little minced parsley; put a little oil into the omelet pan, and when hot pour in the mixture. Cook a few minutes. Insert a knife between the omelet and pan, and with a sudden turn of the hand fold the omelet in two. Finish cooking in hot oven two or three seconds. Serve hot.

GLUTEN OMELET

Same as plain omelet, adding one tablespoonful of gluten to eggs and cream before whipping. Serve at once on a hot platter.

RICE OMELET

Same as plain omelet, only adding one tablespoonful of cooked rice to eggs and milk before beating. Serve on a hot platter at once.

APPLE OMELET

Same as plain omelet. Serve with a tablespoonful of well seasoned apple sauce, mixed with equal amount of beaten white of egg on side of platter.

GRANOSE OMELET

Same as plain omelet, adding two tablespoonfuls of cream instead of milk, and one or two tablespoonfuls of granose, before whipping.

OMELET WITH TOMATO

Prepare a plain omelet, and when ready to fold, put a layer of baked ripe tomatoes on one half, and fold the other half over it. Serve with or without a tomato gravy as preferred.

ONION OMELET

Make as for plain omelet, placing one dessert-spoonful of lightly braized onion on the omelet just before you fold, folding the one-third over the onion. Serve on hot platter at once.

GREEN PEA OMELET

Make as for plain omelet, folding one tablespoonful French peas with a little thick cream sauce over them. Serve at once on hot platter.

ASPARAGUS OMELET

Make as for plain omelet, folding in one tablespoonful of asparagus tips, which have been nicely seasoned. Serve on hot platter at once.

EGG A LA MODE

Bread crumbs, 2 cups.
Milk, 2 cups.
Eggs, 8.
Salt.
Buttered toast or zwieback.

Soak bread crumbs in milk, beat eggs very light, add the soaked bread crumbs, and bake for five minutes. Have ready a hot oiled or buttered saucepan; pour in the mixture, salt, and stir briskly for three minutes. Serve hot on squares of buttered toast or zwieback.

CURDLED EGGS

Bring a kettle of water to a boil, set at back of

range for two minutes, then drop in two eggs for
each person, and leave for eight minutes. Serve in
cups.

JELLIED EGGS

Cook the same as curdled eggs, leaving eggs in
fifteen minutes instead of eight.

SHIRRED EGGS

Oil a small platter or granite egg dish, break in
fresh eggs, being careful not to break the yolks.
Sprinkle with minced parsley, salt, and add a bit of
butter. Set in oven and bake till cooked as desired.
Serve at once.

CREAM SHIRRED EGGS

Prepare eggs as for shirred eggs, omitting parsley.
Pour about one tablespoonful of rich cream over
them, salt, set in oven, and bake as desired. Serve
at once.

FLOATED EGGS

Take two fresh eggs, separate whites from yolks,
put yolks into a soup bowl of hot water, being careful not to break them. Let set two minutes, then
place them, bowl and all, into a larger dish of boiling water, and cook till set as desired,—two minutes
for medium, four minutes for hard. Meantime beat
whites very stiff, mold them in a soup bowl, then
float mold on boiling water two or three minutes
till nicely set. Then place them on large platter,

place yolk in center, garnish with parsley, and serve. In removing whites from bowl, take bowl in left hand, knife in right, dip bowl about one-third in water, then slip knife under edge of mold in the water. The water will get under eggs and float them out easily. This makes a nice dish for the sick, if yolks be boiled hard and whites are cooked rare.

BAKED EGGS IN TOMATO CASES

Take nice, ripe, medium-sized tomatoes, remove the stem and center with sharp paring knife or spoon sufficient to encase an egg nicely. Place them in an oiled granite baking-pan, break an egg into each tomato, salt and sprinkle with chopped parsley, and add a small piece of butter. Set in moderate oven and bake till eggs are medium done. Serve at once.

MUMBLED EGGS

Milk, 1 cup.
Eggs, 6.
Granose biscuit, 3.
Salt.

Put milk on to heat in agate pan; when it begins to boil, break in the eggs, and with a fork stir rapidly till it thickens. It must not be as hard as scrambled eggs. Split granose biscuit in half and heat them in the oven a few minutes. Serve a spoonful of the mumbled eggs on each half of the biscuits. Do not forget to add salt.

SCRAMBLED EGGS WITH SUGAR CORN

Prepare as for scrambled eggs with protose, using nice, tender corn in place of protose. Salt and serve at once on hot platters.

SCRAMBLED EGGS WITH ONIONS

Prepare as for scrambled eggs with protose, using one teaspoonful of lightly braized onion in place of protose. Salt, and serve on hot platters at once.

SCRAMBLED EGGS WITH PROTOSE

Cream or milk, 1 tablespoonful (for one person).
Fresh eggs, 2.
Minced protose, 1 tablespoonful.

Into an oiled skillet containing one tablespoonful of cream or milk break the eggs, slightly whipping them with egg whip or spoon, then add protose. Stir to prevent sticking to bottom, also to thoroughly mix egg with protose. Salt, scramble (soft medium, or hard), as desired. Serve at once on hot platters.

SCRAMBLED EGGS WITH PARSLEY

Prepare as for scrambled eggs with protose, omitting protose and substituting minced parsley.

POACHED EGGS ON TOAST

Serve poached eggs on nice light brown slices of zwieback, or fresh toast if preferred, that has been slightly moistened, not soaked, with hot cream, milk, or water.

POACHED EGGS

Take nice, fresh eggs, as only fresh eggs poach nicely; break them into a pan of hot water, almost boiling. Let pan set on range so that it will not boil; poach as desired,—soft, two minutes; medium, three minutes; hard, five minutes. Serve on platter, garnish with watercress or parsley. Serve while very hot.

POACHED EGGS ON GRANOSE

Heat some granose in the oven a few minutes; put a few spoonfuls on a plate and place poached eggs on top. A small piece of butter may be added to each egg.

BEVERAGES

CARAMEL-CEREAL

(A Substitute for Coffee)

For each cup of the beverage required use two tablespoonfuls of the cereal and boil for ten to twenty minutes. Then remove to the side of the range and let steep a few minutes. The strength and aroma of cereal coffee are developed by long steeping.

CHOCOLATE

(Sanitas)

Grate some Sanitas chocolate, place in a saucepan, and to each two ounces allow one cup of cold water. Let it stand until the chocolate is soft, place over the fire, and when it boils, cook one minute. Work it briskly with an egg beater, then serve at once, adding at the last moment a tablespoonful of whipped cream to each cup.

It is considered an improvement by some to use two-thirds chocolate and one-third malted nuts.

Other chocolate is not recommended, as it contains an injurious alkaloid, which in the Sanitas brand is removed by a special process.

FRUIT NECTAR

For every eight parts of fruit juice used add one part of lemon juice and sweeten to taste. A combination of fruit juices, as grape, cherry, and raspberry, makes a very nice nectar, always using the lemon juice. The nectar should be served ice cold.

STRAWBERRY SHERBET

Ripe strawberries, crushed, 4 cups.
Water, 4 cups.
Lemon, sliced very thin, 1.
Powdered sugar, 2 cups.

Mix the strawberries, water, and lemon together, and let stand in glass or earthen jar for two hours; strain through coarse cloth and add the powdered sugar. When sugar is dissolved strain and keep on the ice until served.

MINT JULEP

Sugar, 1 cup.
Mint sprigs, 6.
Strawberry juice, ½ cup.
Juice of 4 lemons.
Water, 1 pint.
Boiling water, 1 cup.
Raspberry juice, ½ cup.
Ice.

Boil sugar and water twenty minutes; crush mint and pour over it one cup boiling water. Let stand five or ten minutes, strain, and pour into the syrup. To this add strawberry, raspberry, and lemon juices. Serve ice cold.

FRUIT CUPS

Lemons, juice and rind, 12.
Powdered sugar, 2½ pounds.
Ice.
Ripe pineapple, 1.
Water, 2 quarts.

Put into a dish the juice of the lemons and the rind sliced very thin. Slice the pineapple into another dish and pour over it half a pound of the powdered sugar. Let stand overnight. In the morning strain off the juices and add the rest of the sugar and the water. Stir till the sugar is dissolved, then strain through a coarse cloth, and serve with crushed ice.

LEMONADE NO. 1

The best lemonade is made from lemon syrup. Into the juice of twelve lemons grate the rind of six. Be careful to exclude all seeds and the inner white skin, as they impart a bitter taste. Let stand overnight. Make thick syrup of white sugar, and when cold strain the lemon juice into it. A tablespoonful added to a glass of water makes a perfect lemonade.

LEMONADE NO. 2

Three lemons to a pint of water makes a strong lemonade. Sweeten to taste.

ORANGEADE

Sugar, 1 cup.
Water, 2 cups.
Orange juice, 2 cups.
Cracked ice.

Boil sugar and water together ten minutes to make a syrup; then add the orange juice and let it cool. When cold, pour into goblets half filled with cracked ice.

APOLLINARIS LEMONADE

Juice of 6 lemons.
Rind of 4 lemons, sliced very thin.
Sugar, 2 cups.
Apollinaris water, ice cold, ¼ bottle.
Cracked ice.

Mix the lemon juice, rind of the lemons, and sugar together and add Apollinaris water. Serve in goblets of cracked ice.

PINEAPPLE LEMONADE

Sugar, 1 cup.
Water, 2 cups.
Ice water, about 4 cups.
Juice of 4 lemons.
Pineapple, freshly grated, 1.

Boil the sugar and water together ten minutes, and then add lemon juice and freshly-grated pineapple. Let this cool, then strain carefully, and add ice-water, about four cups.

CEREALS

CEREALS

Grains may be considered perfect food in themselves, as they contain all the food elements in nearly right proportions. Rice is an exception to this, the starch being in excess.

In cooking grains in the form of porridges, they should be introduced into rapidly salted water, beating with a batter whisk so that the grains may be thoroughly mixed with the water and be free from lumps. In cooking coarse grains, as cracked wheat, pearl barley, hominy, etc., keep them boiling, stirring occasionally until the grain does not sink to the bottom, but hangs suspended in the water. If the inner part of a double boiler has been used, it may now be set into the outer boiler, which should be placed on the range where the water will boil rapidly. Replenish the water in the outside boiler from time to time with boiling water.

By setting the grain in boiling water, the indigestible outer portion or cellulose is more completely broken up, and the starch granules are more thoroughly acted upon by the water, the object being to cook the starch and the gluten as thoroughly as possible. If the grains are cooked in a double boiler, they will not need to be stirred after they are set, except when cooked in a very large quantity. The cooking should be continuous and the length of time varies according to the varying proportion of gluten in the grain. The larger percentage of starch, the shorter the time required in cooking. Grains combine nicely with fruits, and may be cooked or served with either fruit or fruit juices.

OATMEAL

Oatmeal, 1 cup.
Water, 1 quart.

Put water into a double boiler, place on the range, and when boiling add oatmeal. Boil until it thickens and finish in double boiler. Cook five hours.

ROLLED OATS

Rolled oats, 1½ cups.
Water, 1 quart.

Put water into a double boiler, place on the range, and when boiling add rolled oats. Boil until it thickens and finish in double boiler. Cook four hours.

CRACKED WHEAT

Water, 4 cups.
Salt, 1 teaspoonful.
Cracked wheat, 1 cup.

Put water into the inner double boiler, place on the range, and when boiling add salt and cracked wheat. Boil rapidly until grains do not sink when the dish is lifted from the range. Place in the outer boiler and cook constantly for four or five hours.

PEARL WHEAT

Water, 4 cups.
Pearl wheat, washed, 1 cup.
Salt.

Boil water in the inner double boiler, add pearl wheat, and salt. Place in the outer boiler and cook five or six hours.

PEARL BARLEY

Pearl barley, well washed, 1 cup.
Water, 4 cups.

Put cold water into double boiler and add pearl barley. Heat slowly and cook about six hours.

FARINA

Milk, or water, 6 cups.
Farina, 1 cup.
Salt.

Put the milk or water in the inner part of a double boiler, place on the range, and when boiling add salt and farina. Let it boil for two or three minutes, stirring all the time. Then place in a double boiler and cook one hour. If milk is used, it should first be simmered or scalded in a double boiler, and then placed on the range and the milk will boil almost immediately. In this way the milk will not be so liable to scorch as if it was put on the range at first. This rule will apply to all grains cooked with milk.

RICE (SOUTHERN STYLE)

> Rice, 1 cup.
> Salt, 1 teaspoonful.
> Water, 6 cups.
> Butter or gravy.

Wash rice in two waters, then put into vessel with water and salt. After boiling about ten minutes, strain off all the water except a scant cupful. Cover the vessel and let steam fifteen minutes or more, stirring once or twice. Serve with butter or gravy, the latter being stirred in quickly while the rice is hot.

RICE (WESTERN STYLE)

> Rice, 1 cup.
> Water, 6 cups.
> Salt, 1 tablespoonful.

Wash rice, put in kettle of water, salt, and boil till tender, stirring once or twice to prevent sticking. Drain off all water through a colander and pour over hot water sufficient to wash off the starchy water and separate the grains. Leave in the colander and set into another pan, so that the bottom of colander will not touch. Cover and place in the oven a few minutes.

RICE WITH RAISINS

Washed rice, 1 cup.
Raisins, washed, seeded, ½ cup.
Salt, ½ teaspoonful.
Water, 2 cups.

Put in an enameled pan, cover, and steam one hour.

BROWNED RICE

Rice may be browned in the oven until of a yellow straw color, then cooked as any rice, but preferably steamed. Care must be taken in browning that it does not scorch or get too brown.

CORN MEAL MUSH

Salted water, 4 cups.
Corn meal, 1 cup.

Into the salted water stir corn meal till it begins to thicken, and finish cooking in a double boiler. Cook three or four hours.

GRAHAM PORRIDGE

Graham flour, 1 cup.
Boiling water, salted, 3 cups.

Stir the flour into boiling water and beat till perfectly smooth; set in a double boiler, or in another vessel containing boiling water, and cook one hour.

GRAHAM PORRIDGE WITH DATES

Set as for plain graham porridge; after it has cooked one-half hour, beat in the desired quantity of washed, seeded, and chopped dates; let it cook half an hour longer, and serve.

GLUTEN-GRANOLA MUSH

Boiling milk or water, 1 quart.
Mixed gluten and granola, 1½ pints.

Cook fifteen minutes. and serve with cream.

TOASTS

TOASTS

Toasts are uniformly and properly regarded as a breakfast dish, and when properly prepared are wholesome, nutritious, and appetizing, and far more conducive to health than the fried mushes and griddle cakes with which so many are prone to appease their appetites.

Zwieback should be used as the foundation of all toasts, although ordinary toasted bread can be used. In toasting bread, do not expose it to such fierce heat that the bread will be burned or singed. Singed bread is not toasted bread. Again, the fire should be hot enough to more than simply dry the bread. It should be toasted as far through as possible, and should be crisp and brittle, not hard. In using zwieback for toast it may be moistened by hot milk, if for cream, gravy, or egg toast; or with hot salted water, if for fruit. In either case the toast should be dipped quickly in and out again so as not to absorb too much liquid and become mushy. Under this head a few kinds of toasts will be given, inexpensive and otherwise. While it is not an exhaustive list, it will include sufficient to suggest others equally good.

MILK TOAST

Milk, 6 cups.
Flour, 1 heaped teaspoonful.
Butter, 1 tablespoonful.
Toasted bread or zwieback.

Heat milk and butter in a saucepan over the fire; when boiling, add salt and flour, moistened with a little milk. Let it boil, remove from the fire, and dip into this slices of toasted bread or zwieback. Pour what remains over the toast, cover, and send to the table hot.

CREAM TOAST

Cream, 6 cups.
Zwieback.
Milk.

Heat cream to boiling, dip slices of zwieback into hot milk for an instant, place on saucer, pour hot cream over, and serve.

AMERICAN OR FRENCH TOAST

Eggs, thoroughly beaten, 3.
Salt.
Butter.
Milk, 3 cups.
Sliced bread.

Beat the eggs thoroughly and add the milk and a little salt. Slice light bread and dip into the mixture, allowing each slice to absorb some of the milk. Then brown on a hot, buttered griddle or thick bottomed frying-pan. Spread with butter, and serve hot.

BOSTON CREAM TOAST

Toast two slices of bread, trim and cut in two lengthwise, making four pieces. Place these evenly on top of one another and cut again cornerwise, into long triangular pieces. Arrange artistically on a platter, and serve with cream sauce.

NUN'S TOAST

Hard-boiled eggs, 6.
Flour, 1 teaspoonful.
Butter.
Hot buttered toast.
Finely-chopped onion, 1.
Milk, 2 cups.

Put the butter into a saucepan, and when it begins to bubble add the chopped onion. Let the onion cook a little without color, then stir in the flour. Add the milk and stir till it becomes smooth. Then put in the eggs which have been sliced and let them get hot. Pour this mixture over neatly trimmed slices of hot, buttered toast. Season with salt.

NUT GRAVY TOAST

Dress moistened toast with nut gravy as given under sauces.

PRUNE WHIPPED TOAST

Prune pulp, 2 cups.
Sugar, 1 tablespoonful.
Eggs, whites, 4.

Beat the whites very stiff and stir in the hot prune pulp and sugar. Serve on slices of zwieback which have been dipped in hot water.

PRUNE TOAST

Prepare as for apricot toast, using prune marmalade.

DATE TOAST

Prepare as for prune toast, except that the dates should be steamed, not boiled.

PROTOSE TOAST

Minced protose, 2 cups.
Eggs, 2.
Sweet cream, ½ cup.
Salt to taste.

Mix and heat thoroughly; when boiling hot spread over slices of

Toasted bread.

Dipped in hot salt water, and well buttered. Take

Hard-boiled egg, 1,

Cut in halves, remove yolk, and fill hole with

Currant jelly,

And place on top of the protose.

NUTTOLENE ON TOAST

Mince half a pound of nuttolene very fine, put in a well-oiled saucepan, and fry over the fire till a delicate brown. Great care must be taken to prevent scorching; shake the pan often. Make two cups of rich cream sauce well seasoned with butter sauce, and desiccated cocoanut. Strain this over the nuttolene, and serve a spoonful on warm toast. This makes six large portions.

BERRY TOAST

Any canned fruit, as strawberries, blackberries. blueberries, etc., may be used for toasts. Strain off the juice, boil, and thicken with corn starch to the consistency of cream. Stir in the strawberries and reheat till the berries are well heated through. Serve as other fruit toasts.

BANANA TOAST NO. 1

Peel and rub some nice bananas through a fine colander; sweeten and beat up with a little cream, and serve on moistened toast. Serve cold.

BANANA TOAST NO. 2

Take the desired quantity of bright fruit juice, as strawberry or cherry. Boil and thicken with corn starch. Into this slice some ripe bananas. The juice should not be too thick, but just so that the banana will appear suspended in the juice. Serve on moistened toast.

DATE TOAST WITH WALNUTS

Prepare same as date toast, then serve with walnut meat on each corner and one in the center.

TOMATO TOAST

Dress moistened toast with tomato sauce, as given under sauces; or use strained tomatoes thickened with flour or corn starch.

ASPARAGUS TOAST

Prepare as for stewed asparagus. Moisten and butter a piece of toast, lay four or five pieces of asparagus on it, pour a spoonful of white sauce on the bottom end of the stalks, and serve.

APPLE TOAST

Fresh stewed apples, rubbed through a colander and sweetened, make a nice dressing. The apples may be flavored with lemon, or mixed with grape or cranberry sauce. When the apples are put in the colander, the liquid may be poured into a saucepan and boiled into a syrup, and the toast moistened with this. Serve a spoonful or two of the apple sauce over all.

APRICOT TOAST

In making apricot marmalade, save the juice by itself and boil it down into a syrup. Moisten the toast, pour over some of the syrup, and some of the marmalade over all.

BAKERY AND BREAKFAST DISHES

BAKERY AND BREAKFAST DISHES

Thin batters are about the consistency of thin cream. Thick batters are like cream. Still thicker batters, which may be poured in a continuous stream, are called pour batters. Any batter is a pour batter until it is made so stiff that it breaks or drops in the pouring, when it is called a drop batter. It will remain a batter until too stiff to be beaten, when it becomes a dough.

Doughs, like batters, are of varying degrees of thickness, ranging from those just stiff enough to be handled to those which may be rolled thin as paper. Generally speaking, one full measure of flour to one scant measure of liquid makes a pour batter. Two full measures of flour make a drop batter; and three full measures make a dough; although, for various reasons, these proportions are subject to many modifications.

If the ingredients in batters were simply mixed and cooked slowly, the resulting substances would be hard and compact, unfit for human digestion. Hence, to obviate this, and to make them light and porous, we must resort to other processes. This is accomplished by means of the expansion of incorporated air, by the generation of gas within the mixture, or by a combination of both methods, supplemented by quick cooking before the gas has a chance to escape.

Air at seventy degrees expands to about three

times its volume when exposed to the temperature of a hot oven. Consequently, as a mixture heats in cooking, incorporated air expands, giving the desired lightness. Air is incorporated or enclosed in batters by beating the mixture thoroughly, as in making whole-wheat gems; by adding eggs to the beaten mixture, as in popovers; and by the gas obtained by the union of an acid with an alkaline carbonate, as in the use of baking powders. In batters made light by the admixture of air, one must exercise care in beating to actually incorporate and retain the air. When eggs are added to the mixture, the glutinous consistency of the albumin they contain assists in retaining the entangled air.

GEMS OR PUFFS (PLAIN)

Milk, 1 cup.
Salt.
Cooking oil, 1 tablespoonful, if desired.
Egg, 1.
Sifted flour, about 2 cups.

Break the egg into the milk, add salt, and beat thoroughly. Beat into this enough sifted flour to make a batter that will pile slightly when poured in a thick stream. Bake in hot greased gem irons in a brisk oven. A tablespoonful of cooking oil may be added to the milk if a richer batter is desired.

CORN GEMS

Make same as plain gems, but use one-fourth corn meal and a little sugar.

WHOLE-WHEAT AND GRAHAM GEMS

Use one-fourth to one-third whole wheat or graham flour.

GRANOSE PUFFS

Eggs, 4.
Ground cinnamon, 1 teaspoonful.
Salt.
Sugar, ¼ cup.
Granose flakes, 4 cups.

Beat the yolks of the eggs with the sugar until light, then add the cinnamon and salt. Beat again, then add two cups granose flakes. Mix thoroughly and add half of the stiffly-beaten whites of the eggs, then two more cups granose flakes, and lastly the rest of the whites. Drop in round gem irons, filling them heaping full, and bake a light brown. They may be iced and a little shredded cocoanut sprinkled on top.

VEGETARIAN HOT CAKES

Bread crumbs, 4 cups.
Flour, 1 cup.
Salt, 1 teaspoonful.
Sugar as desired.

Mix all together thoroughly, and add sufficient
Milk heated at 140° or 150°,
To make a thick pour batter. To this add the
yolks of 5 eggs.
Beat up thoroughly and add the
Stiffly-beaten whites.
Bake on soapstone griddle. Be careful not to

have the milk scalding hot, as it renders cakes soft
and sticky.

GREEN CORN GRIDDLE CAKES

Corn, 1 quart, cut from the ear.
Butter, 2 tablespoonfuls.
White corn meal, 3 tablespoonfuls.
Salt, ¼ teaspoonful.
Milk, 1 cup.
Eggs, 4.
Flour, ½ cup.

Mix thoroughly and bake on soapstone griddle.

BAKED CORN PIE

Sweet corn, 1 can.
Milk, 2 cups.
Salt, 1 teaspoonful.
Butter, 2 tablespoonfuls.
Eggs, 2.

Warm the butter and stir through the corn; beat
the eggs with the milk, add the salt, and mix with
the butter and the corn. Turn into a pan and bake
until set. Should be light brown.

POPOVERS

Flour, 2 cups.
Milk, 1¾ cups.
Butter.
Salt, ½ level teaspoonful.
Eggs, 3.

Mix the salt and flour, pour on slowly half the milk to make a smooth batter; add the eggs, one at a time, beating well, and gradually the remaining milk. Beat vigorously for a few minutes, then turn at once into hot well-buttered gem-pans, filling them about half full. Bake in rather hot oven from twenty to thirty minutes.

CORN BREAD WITHOUT BAKING POWDER
NO. 1

> Corn meal, 2 cups.
> Eggs, 4.
> Salt.
> Boiling milk, 3 cups.
> Butter, size of egg.

Put the meal into the mixing bowl, make hollow in the center, put in butter and salt, and pour the hot milk over all, and stir well. Let cool, and if too stiff, add a little more cold milk. Break the eggs and separate them; add the yolks to the meal and beat five minutes. Beat the whites and add them to the batter. Oil a baking-pan, make it hot, and turn in the batter. Bake in a quick oven thirty minutes.

HOE CAKE

> Corn meal, 4 cups.
> Water, or milk.
> Melted butter, 1 tablespoonful.
> Salt and sugar as desired.

Sift corn meal with a little salt, and sugar if desired; scald with sufficient water or milk to make a stiff batter, but soft enough to spread easily with a knife. A tablespoonful of melted butter may be added if desired. Spread on a baking-sheet or pan about one-half inch thick or less and bake slowly till crisp clear through.

If the cake bakes fast on the bottom, it may be turned over so that both sides may be evenly baked.

CORN BREAD WITHOUT BAKING POWDER NO. 2

Corn meal, 2 cups.
Flour, 1 cup.
Salt, 1 teaspoonful.
Sugar, ¼ cup.

Mix and add

Boiling water.

sufficient to make stiff dough; let cool, then stir in

Butter, 1 tablespoonful.
Beaten yolks, 6.

and lastly the

Stiffly-beaten whites, 6.

CORN BREAD NO. 3

Sponge, 3 cups.
Butter, 1 rounded tablespoonful.
Mixture, 2 parts corn meal to 1 part flour.
Eggs, 2.
Sugar, 3 heaped tablespoonfuls.

Take three cups of the sponge as set for making wheat bread, measured when light, ready to mix up stiff. Add sugar, eggs, and butter. To this add a mixture of two-thirds corn meal and one-third flour until it is as stiff as will stir conveniently (if made too stiff, the bread will be dry; if not stiff enough, it will be sticky). Put about half an inch deep in greased pans, and let rise till nearly an inch deep and bake in a moderate oven. It may be in deeper loaves, but they are not likely to be so satisfactory.

GEORGIA PONES

> Southern corn meal, 2 cups.
> Sugar, 1 tablespoonful.
> Salt, ½ teaspoonful.
> Boiling milk or cream.

Sift meal with sugar and salt. Pour over this enough boiling milk or cream to make a stiff drop batter. Stir constantly, that the meal may not lump. When perfectly smooth, drop in large spoonfuls on a cold buttered baking-sheet and bake in a brisk oven. The pones should be browned on top.

BOSTON BROWN BREAD

> Yellow corn meal, 1 cup.
> White flour, ¾ cup.
> Salt, 1 teaspoonful.
> Eggs, 4.
> Graham flour, 1 cup.
> New Orleans molasses (good), ¾ cup.
> Milk, about 3 cups.

Mix meal, flour, molasses, and milk; separate eggs and mix yolks with other ingredients. Beat whites very stiff and fold into mixture, which should not be thick. Put this in the tin dish immediately and steam for three or four hours.

PUDDINGS

LEMON-APPLE

Tart apples, 6
Sugar, 1 cup.
Lemon, 1.

Pare the apples and remove the core, being careful not to break the apple. Put into a granite or enameled baking-pan of suitable size. Fill the hole made by removing the cores, with the sugar; moisten the sugar with the lemon juice and sprinkle a little of the grated rind on each apple. Pour sufficient water into the pan to half cover the apples. Cover and bake until clear.

FARINA MOLD

Milk, 1 quart.
Sugar, ⅓ cup.
Farina, ½ cup.
Salt.

Put the milk into double boiler; when scalding hot, set the inner boiler on range until the milk boils; then stir in the farina, sugar, and salt. Let boil till the farina is set, then set back in outer boiler and cook one hour. Turn into molds previously oiled or dipped into cold water. May be served with cream sweetened and flavored, or with fruit juice.

BROWN BETTY

Chopped apples, 2 cups.
Bread crumbs, 1 cup.
Butter, ½ cup.
Chopped raisins, 1 cup.
Raisin or prune juice, 1 cup.

Fill a pudding dish with alternate layers of the fruit, crumbs, and butter,—fruit first, finishing bread crumbs on top. Pour over the fruit juice. Set the dish in a pan of hot water; cover and bake in a moderate oven for nearly an hour; then remove the cover and brown lightly. Serve with sweetened cream or lemon sauce.

STRAWBERRY SHORT CAKE

Cream, 1 cup.
Flour to make a medium soft dough.
Salt.
Yeast, 1 tablespoonful.

Warm the cream to about seventy degrees, add the salt, yeast, and about two cups of the flour. Mix thoroughly, cover, and set in a warm place to rise. When well risen and lively, add the rest of the flour, and leave until perfectly smooth. Roll out about half an inch thick. Put in greased pans, brush the top with melted butter, let rise until about double its original size, and bake. Split, and fill with whole or crushed berries, sprinkled with sugar.

STRAWBERRY GRANOSE

Put a layer of granose in a deep pan of sufficient size; cover with a layer of crushed berries and sugar; repeat till the pan is full. Press lightly. Serve with cream.

FLOATING ISLAND

Milk, 1 quart.
Sugar, ½ cup.
Eggs, 5.
Jelly, 2 tablespoonfuls.
Flavor to suit.

Make a custard with the milk, the yolks of the eggs, the whites of two, and the sugar. Whip the remaining three whites to a stiff froth with a little sugar and flavoring, same as custard. Pour the custard into individual glass dishes, drop spoonfuls of the whites on the custard so as to form islands, or it may be put on with a pastry tube or paper funnel. Drop a little bright jelly in the center of each island.

CORN STARCH BLANC MANGE

Milk, 1 quart.
Corn starch, 4 heaped tablespoonfuls.
Eggs, whites, 3.
Sugar, ½ cup.
Lemon flavoring.

Put half the milk in a double boiler and set over the fire. When scalding hot, add the remaining milk in which has been dissolved the sugar and corn starch. Stir till it is thick and there are no lumps. Flavor with lemon, take from the range, and add the stiffly beaten whites. Pour into molds and set in a cool place to get firm.

A pleasing effect may be obtained by dividing the mixture after it is cooked, and coloring one-half pink, then filling the mold one-third of one, and filling up with the other. When turned from the mold they will look like small, white pyramids capped with pink, or pink with white. A custard to be served with this blanc mange is made of two cups of milk, the yolks of three eggs, and half a cup of sugar. Flavor same as blanc mange.

GRANOSE MOLD

Boiling milk, 2 cups.
Granose flakes, 3 cups.
Sugar, 2 tablespoonfuls.
Beaten eggs, 6.

Stir the granose flakes into the boiling milk; then add the beaten eggs and sugar. Let boil two minutes, and pour into molds. Serve with vanilla sauce.

PINEAPPLE TAPIOCA

Pearl tapioca, 1 cup.
Pineapple, ripe, 1.
Water, 1 quart.
Sugar, 1 cup.

Wash the tapioca, and put to cook with the water and sugar in a double boiler; cook until cleared.

Pare the pineapple, remove the core, and slice very thin. Put a layer of the pineapple in a deep pan; pour over some of the tapioca, then another layer of pineapple, and so on till all the pineapple and tapioca are used. Serve cold.

BANANA TAPIOCA

Same as pineapple tapioca, but use bananas instead of pineapples. Milk may be substituted for water, and two eggs used if desired.

The tapioca may be flavored and colored if desired.

DATES STUFFED WITH MALTED NUTS

Wash, dry, and pit the desired quantity of dates, being careful not to break more than are necessary. Fill the cavity made by removing the pit with malted nuts, and press together. Make an icing of the white of an egg, eight or nine tablespoonfuls of powdered sugar, a few drops of lemon juice, and one teaspoonful of corn starch. Dip the dates in this, using a sharp toothpick with which to handle them, and place on an oiled paper or plate to dry. Or the icing may be made with less sugar, and after they are dipped, roll them in powdered or Victor sugar.

SAGO FRUIT

Sago, 1 cup.
Sugar, ½ cup.
Oranges, 2.

14

Wash the sago through three waters, and simmer in a quart of water with the sugar until transparent and thoroughly done. Peel and slice the oranges, remove the pips, and add to the sago. Cook a few minutes longer, then turn into six or eight individual glass sauce dishes, and put away to cool. Garnish with a little bright colored jelly or jam.

RICE PATTIES

Rice, cooked, 2 cups.
Butter, 1½ tablespoonfuls.
Egg whites, well-beaten, 2
Sugar, 1 tablespoonful.
Nutmeg.

Mix, and stir over the fire till well blended; when cold, form into patties, roll in beaten white of egg, and then in bread crumbs moistened with melted butter. Bake. Serve hot with sweetened cream, flavored with nutmeg.

LEMON OMELET

Corn starch, 1 dessertspoonful.
Cream, ½ cup.
Eggs, 4.
Butter.
Powdered sugar.
Flour, 1 teaspoonful.
Salt.
Boiling milk, 1 cup.
Lemon honey.

Mix the corn starch, flour, cream and salt. Beat till smooth; add the beaten yolks of the eggs and the boiling milk. Stir in the whites of the eggs, beaten to a stiff froth. Butter four pudding plates, pour in the mixture, and bake in a quick oven ten minutes. Spread lemon honey on half, fold over, and sprinkle powdered sugar on top. Serve hot.

LEMON HONEY

White sugar, 1 cup.
Egg yolks, 3.
Butter, 1 tablespoonful.
Lemon, grated rind and juice of 1.
Egg white, 1.

Put the juice, sugar, and butter in a double boiler over the fire; while it is melting, beat the eggs and add to them the grated rind of the lemon. Add this to the sugar and butter, cooking and stirring till it is thick and clear like honey.

STRAWBERRY SOUFFLE

Fruit.
Fresh strawberries, 3 quarts.
Powdered sugar, 1½ cups.
Custard.
Egg yolks, 4.
Cream or milk, ¾ pint.
Sugar.
Meringue.
Egg whites, 4.

Put two and a half quarts of the strawberries and the powdered sugar into a saucepan. Put in oven and let it simmer till sugar is melted. Beat the yolks of the eggs in the cream or milk, and sweeten to taste. Set in double boiler over the fire, and stir till thick. Arrange the berries without the juice in glass dishes, so that they will form a sort of wall. Fill the center with custard and meringue the top with the whites. Use the remaining two cups of berries to decorate the meringue with half or whole berries. Serve hot or cold.

PLAIN CUSTARD

Sugar, ¾ cup.
Eggs, 6.
Milk, 1 quart.
Salt.

Beat the eggs till light, and stir in the milk, sugar, and salt. Bake in a pudding-pan; set in a pan of hot water. Bake until the center of custard is set.

CARAMEL CUSTARD

Milk, 3 cups.
Butter, 1 tablespoonful.
Water, ½ cup.
Sugar, 1 cup.
Eggs, 6.
Vanilla, ½ teaspoonful.

Put the butter into a saucepan and set on the range. When melted, stir in the sugar, and let cook until of a dark brown color, stirring frequently to prevent burning. Now add the water, which should be hot, and stir until the caramel (the browned sugar) is dissolved Beat up the eggs and mix with the milk: add this to the caramel and flavor with the vanilla. Pour into custard cups, set into a shallow pan of water, and bake till the custard is set in the middle.

TAPIOCA CUSTARD (RICH)

Tapioca, ½ cup.
Sugar, ¾ cup.
Salt, ¼ teaspoonful.
Milk, 1 quart.
Eggs, 4.
Flavor to suit.

Wash the tapioca and put to cook with the milk in a double boiler; stir occasionally, and cook till clear. Beat the eggs till light; beat in the sugar, and add to the tapioca. Let cook a minute and remove from the range. Stir in the flavoring, and turn into a pan of suitable size. Serve cold. If desired, the whites of two of the eggs may be used as a meringue, which should be flavored the same as the custard.

RICE PUDDING

Rice, 4 tablespoonfuls.
Sugar, 2 tablespoonfuls.
Seedless raisins, ½ cup.
Milk, 4 cups.
Grated nutmeg, ¼ teaspoonful.
Salt, ½ teaspoonful.

Put all together and bake about two hours. Stir with a fork three or four times during first hour to prevent sticking. Should it get too dry, add a little more milk.

CREAM RICE PUDDING

Washed rice, ½ cup.
Cream, or milk, 3 cups.
Eggs, 4.

Cook the rice in the cream or milk; when nearly done, remove from the range, and stir in the yolks of the eggs. Pour into a pan, and set in another containing water, and bake fifteen or twenty minutes, or till the eggs are cooked. Make a meringue of the whites.

SANITAS CHOCOLATE PUDDING

Bread crumbs, 2 cups.
Eggs, 3.
Sanitas chocolate, ¼ pound.
Hot milk, 2 cups.
Sugar, ⅓ cup.

Soak bread crumbs in hot milk, add eggs, sugar, and chocolate. Beat the eggs and mix all the ingredients thoroughly. Put into a buttered can, and steam two hours.

See note under "Beverages, Sanitas Chocolate."

APPLE NUT PUDDING

Apple pulp, 2 cups.
Nuttolene, ½ pound.
Eggs, 4.
Sugar, ¾ cup.
Bread crumbs, 1¾ pounds.
Cinnamon or nutmeg, 1 teaspoonful.

Grate sufficient tart apples to make two cups; then add the sugar, cinnamon or nutmeg, bread crumbs, nuttolene, which has been put through a vegetable grinder, and the beaten yolks of the eggs. Beat well and add the stiffly-beaten whites, put into an oiled pudding-pan set in a pan of boiling water, and bake. Serve with sweetened cream or flavored sauce.

PRUNE TAPIOCA PUDDING

Tapioca, ½ cup.
Cold water, 2½ cups.
Lemon juice, 1 tablespoonful.
Prunes, 1 cup.
Salt, ½ teaspoonful.
Sugar, ½ cup.

Put the prunes into enough water to cover them, and let simmer gently till they absorb all the water. Turn onto a plate to cool and remove stones. When tapioca has cooked until clear, put all the seasoning into it, and put a layer into a pudding dish, then a layer of prunes, and so on, having the top layer tapioca. Bake in moderate oven one hour; then allow to partially cool, and serve with cream.

PRUNE PUDDING

Prune pulp, 1 cup.
Prune meats, chopped fine, ¼ cup.
Egg whites, well beaten, 4.
Sugar, ½ cup.

Stir the beaten whites of the eggs with the prune pulp, and add the chopped prune meats and sugar. Bake till lightly browned, and serve with cream.

BREAD PUDDING

Milk, 1 quart.
Sugar, ½ cup.
Stale bread, 1½ cups.
Eggs, 3.
Flavor to suit.

Soak the bread in the milk; beat the yolks and one of the whites of the eggs with the sugar, and flavor. Mix and put into a pudding dish. Set into a pan of hot water and bake until the custard is set. Meringue with the whites.

If desired, the top of the pudding may first be marked with jelly, marmalade, or fresh fruit of some kind, and the meringue put over all.

PRESSED FRUIT PUDDING

Bread, 8 slices.
Stewed huckleberries, 1 quart.
Sugar, ½ cup.

Trim the bread, cutting off all crusts, put four slices in the bottom of a pudding-pan, cover with half the berries, which should have the juice strained off, sprinkle over part of the sugar, then the rest of the bread and the remainder of the berries and sugar. Pour over all the juice that has been drained; there should be enough to moisten the bread thoroughly. If served the same day, put another pan on top of the pudding, with a weight in it, to press the pudding. It is not necessary to press the pudding if not used the same day it is made. Serve with sweetened cream or sweet sauce.

SNOW PUDDING

Milk, 1 quart.
Salt, ⅓ teaspoonful.
Eggs, whites, 5.
Sugar, ⅓ cup.
Corn starch, ⅓ cup.
Vanilla to suit.

Set milk, sugar, and salt in double boiler over the fire; when scalding hot, add the corn starch mixed smooth in a little cold milk. When the starch is cooked, remove from the fire, and beat well. When cold, stir in carefully the stiffly-beaten whites and flavor with vanilla. Serve with vanilla sauce.

APPLE PUDDING (BAKED)

Butter, 2 tablespoonfuls.
Eggs, 4.
Green tart apples, grated, 6.
Sugar, ½ cup.
Lemon, 1.

Stir the butter and sugar to a cream; stir into this the well-beaten yolks of the eggs, the juice and grated rind of the lemon, and the grated apples. Stir in the beaten whites of the eggs, flavor with cinnamon or nutmeg, and bake. Serve cold with cream.

PLUM PUDDING

Eggs, 4.
Cream, 1 cup.
Flour, 1¾ cups.
Raisins, seeded, chopped, ½ pound.
Dried cherries, ½ pound.
Candied orange peel, 2 ounces.
Sugar, 1 cup.
Bread crumbs 1 cup.
Butter, ⅓ pound.
Currants ½ pound.
Candied citron, 2 ounces.

Beat the eggs, add the cream, bread crumbs, flour, and butter. Beat well together, and mix in the sugar and fruit. Mix well, pour into a buttered pan, cover, and steam about two hours.

CABINET PUDDING

Candied citron, ½ cup.
Seedless raisins, ½ cup.
Currants, ½ cup.
Cinnamon.
Nutmeg.
Stale sponge cake, 1 quart.
Milk, 2 cups.
Eggs, 2.
Butter, melted, 1 tablespoonful.
Salt.

Butter a pudding mold that will hold at least two quarts. Have the citron and raisins chopped fine, the currants well washed, and the cake cut into strips about an inch and a half wide and half an inch thick; sprinkle some of the fruit on the bottom of the mold, then slices of the cake; sprinkle on a little cinnamon and nutmeg, then more fruit, then cake, and so on till the ingredients are all used. Pour over this a custard made of the milk, eggs, and melted butter. Pour this over the cake without cooking, and let soak one-half hour, then set into a pan of water, cover, and bake until the custard is set. Serve with a tart sauce.

CREAM SAGO PUDDING

Sago, ½ cup.
Sugar, 1 cup.
Milk or cream, 1 quart.
Eggs, 2.
Lemon flavoring.

Wash the sago, and with the milk put into a double boiler, and cook until clear. Beat the eggs very light, and add the sugar and flavor. Remove the sago from the range, and allow to cool a little, then pour in the eggs and sugar, beating all the time. Put in a pudding-pan, set in a pan of water, cover, and bake until the custard is set.

STEAMED FRUIT PUDDING

Tart apple pulp, 2 cups.
Sugar, 1 cup.
Eggs, 6.
Grape juice, 2½ cups.
Salt, ½ teaspoonful.
Toasted bread crumbs, 4 cups.
Seedless raisins, 1 cup.
Lemon rind, grated, 1.
Vanilla, 1 tablespoonful.

Mix all well together except the whites of the eggs, which should be beaten stiff and added last. Turn into a buttered mold, and steam or boil for three hours. Serve with sweetened cream, flavored with nutmeg.

SPONGE PUDDING

Milk, 2 cups.
Flour, ½ cup.
Sugar, ⅓ cup.
Eggs, 4.

Put milk into a double boiler. Mix the sugar and flour with a little cold milk; pour this into the scalding milk, and stir till it thickens; then stir it into the well-beaten yolks of the eggs; then add the whites beaten stiff. Pour the mixture into buttered cups or into a pudding dish. Put the cup or dish into a pan of boiling water, place in the oven, and bake twenty minutes. About five minutes before it is done, remove from the pan of water, and finish baking on the grate. Serve in the cups in which it is baked or on hot plates if baked in a pudding dish. This should not be allowed to stand, but be served immediately.

FIG PUDDING

Butter, 2 tablespoonfuls.
Corn starch, ½ cup.
Flour, ½ cup.
Fig marmalade, 1¼ cups.
Cream, 1½ cups.
Sugar, 1 cup.
Eggs, 4.

Mix the butter with the corn starch and flour; mix the fig marmalade and the cream; stir in the butter, corn starch, and flour mixture, together with the sugar and the yolks of eggs. Mix well and fold in quickly the well-beaten whites. Pour into a buttered pudding-pan and steam one and one-half hours.

DATE PUDDING

Make same as fig pudding, using date marmalade.

ADELAIDE PUDDING

Eggs, 6.
Water, 2 cups.
Lemon extract, 1 teaspoonful.
Salt, 1 teaspoonful.
Corn starch, 1 cup.
Sugar, 1¼ cups.
Lemon, grated rind and juice, 1.
Flour, 1½ cups.

Over the beaten yolks pour a syrup made by boiling the sugar in the water. Add lemon rind and juice, lemon extract, and salt. Beat up well, and mix in slowly the flour and corn starch. Fold in the beaten whites of the eggs, pour into a greased pudding dish, and steam one and one-half hours.

CEREAL PUDDING

Milk, 4 cups.
Eggs, 4.
Sugar, ½ cup.
Cream of maize, or cerealine, 2 cups.
Lemon, grated rind and juice, 1.

Heat milk to boiling and stir in cream of maize or cerealine. Set in double boiler and cook half an hour. Remove from range and stir in the yolks and sugar. Flavor with grated rind and juice of lemon. Pour in a shallow pan, and set within another containing water, and bake till the custard sets. Meringue with the whites.

PIES

PASTRY DOUGH FOR PIES

Flour, 1 pint.
Butter, 3 tablespoonfuls, rounding full,
    or, Olive oil, ½ cup.
Salt, 1 teaspoonful.
Cold water, 6 tablespoonfuls.

Chop the butter in the flour, add the water and salt, and without mixing turn upon the board. Roll out and double over three times. Then roll out again and double. Continue this till the crust is smooth; then roll out very thin and roll as for jelly cake. Cut into two pieces, stand each piece on end, and roll out one for the top and the other for the bottom crust.

PUMPKIN FOR PIES

Wash the pumpkin, but do not peel; remove the seeds, cut up, cook and put through a colander. The pumpkin is much sweeter cooked this way than when the peel is removed before cooking.

PUMPKIN PIES

Mashed pumpkin, 1 cup.
Molasses, ⅓ cup.
Sugar, ⅓ cup.
Salt, 1 teaspoonful.
Flour, 1 tablespoonful.
Eggs, 2.
Cinnamon, 1 teaspoonful.
Milk, 1 cup.

Mix all together thoroughly, adding the milk last.

15   (225)

PUMPKIN PIES WITHOUT EGGS

Mashed pumpkin, 1 cup.
Flour, 1 tablespoonful.
Sugar, ½ cup.
Nutmeg, a dash.
Mix together, and when smooth, add
Sweet cream, 1 cup.

SANITAS CHOCOLATE CUSTARD PIE NO. 1

Milk, 1 quart.
Sugar, 1 cup.
Eggs, 6.
Chocolate, ¼ pound.
Water, 2 cups.
Vanilla, 2 teaspoonfuls.

Save the whites of three of the eggs for meringue; beat together the remainder of the eggs, sugar, and vanilla; dissolve the chocolate in the water and boil for three minutes. When nearly cold, add to the eggs and sugar. Put in pan lined with good pastry and bake; makes two large or three small pies.

SANITAS CHOCOLATE CUSTARD PIE NO. 2

Make an ordinary custard pie, flavor with vanilla; put the grated chocolate into a basin on the side of the range, where it will melt, but not burn. When melted, beat into it one egg and sugar to suit the taste. Spread on top of the pie.

HYGIENIC MINCE MEAT

(For Six Pies)

Chopped apples, medium size, 14.
Chopped walnuts, 1 cup.
Chopped blanched almonds, ½ cup.
Chopped figs, ½ cup.
Chopped citron, ¼ cup.
Seeded raisins, 1 cup.
Seedless raisins or currants, 1 cup.
Caramel-cereal coffee, 1 cup.
Fruit juice or jelly, 1 cup.
Lemons, juice of, 4.
Salt, 1 tablespoonful.
Sugar and spice to taste.

MINCE PIE

Minced apples, 4 cups.
Prune juice, 1 cup.
Sugar, 1 cup.
Molasses, 1 cup.
Butter, 2 tablespoonfuls.
Minced protose, 3 cups.
Seedless raisins, 2 cups.
Lemon, grated rind and juice, 1.

Stew all together until thick enough for filling.
Flavor with

Salt, 1 teaspoonful.
Cinnamon.
Nutmeg.

BAKER'S CUSTARD PIE

Sugar, 3 tablespoonfuls.
Eggs, 3.
Vanilla, 1 teaspoonful.
Salt to taste.
Flour, 1 tablespoonful.
Milk, 2 cups.
Grated nutmeg.

Beat the yolks of the eggs to a cream, stir the flour thoroughly into the sugar, and add to the eggs. Then put in the vanilla, nutmeg, and salt; then add well-beaten whites. Mix well and add by degrees the milk that has been scalded and cooled (but not boiled), and turn all into a deep pie-pan, lined with rich paste. Bake from twenty-five to thirty minutes.

LEMON PIE (SUPERIOR)

Lemons, 3.
Water, 3 cups.
Corn starch, 2 tablespoonfuls.
Butter, 1 tablespoonful.
Sugar, 2½ cups.
Eggs, 3.
Flour, 4 tablespoonfuls.

Put the water and butter into a double boiler and set on the range. Mix the sugar, flour, and corn starch together; grate in the lemon rind, add the juice and beaten yolks of the eggs. When the water in the boiler is scalding hot, stir in the mixture, and cook till of the consistency of cold honey, stirring now and then to ensure even cooking. Remove from the fire; when cool, pour into deep pie tins, lined with good pastry. When done, meringue with the whites of the eggs.

COCOANUT PIE

Desiccated Cocoanut, ½ cup.
Eggs, 2.
Butter, size of an egg.
Milk, 1 cup.
Sugar, 1 small cup.

Soak the cocoanut in the milk, add the beaten egg, sugar, and butter melted. Line a pie-pan with rich pastry, put in the filling, and bake. The white of one of the eggs may be used as a meringue, if desired.

WASHINGTON CREAM PIE

Crust:
Eggs, 6.
Vanilla, 1 teaspoonful.
Flour, 1 rounded cup.
Sugar, 1 cup.
Lemon juice, 2 teaspoonfuls.

Beat the yolks of the eggs till very thick; add the sugar, vanilla, and lemon juice. Beat the whites of the eggs very stiff, fold half the whites into the

yolk and sugar, then half the flour, then the re-
mainder of the whites and the rest of the flour.
Divide this batter into two pie-pans and bake.
When cold, split each cake and put in the filling.

> Filling:
> Milk, 2 cups.
> Eggs, 2.
> Flour, ½ cup.
> Butter, 2 tablespoonfuls.
> Sugar, 1 cup.
> Vanilla, 1½ teaspoonfuls.

Put three-fourths of the milk into a double boiler,
together with the milk, and set on the range. Beat
the eggs very light; add the sugar, flour, and the
remainder of the milk. Beat till perfectly smooth,
and when the milk in the boiler is scalding hot, stir
in the mixture. Beat till smooth, and cook thoroughly; when cool, add the vanilla. If made a day
or two before serving, and kept on ice, the quality
of these pies is greatly improved.

PRUNE PIE

> Prune, marmalade, 1 pint.
> Egg, 1.
> Lemon, 1.
> Sugar, ½ cup.

To the marmalade add the grated rind and juice
of the lemon, sugar, and beaten yolk of egg; put
into a pie-pan lined with good paste and bake till

the crust is done; remove from oven and meringue
with the white of the egg.

APPLE PIE

Line a pie-pan with rich paste, sprinkle over the
bottom a little flour and sugar. Fill with apples
cut in thin slices. The pan should be slightly
rounding full. Sprinkle a little flour and sugar, according to the tartness of the fruit. Add two tablespoonfuls of water, and a few small pieces of butter.
Moisten the edge of the paste and put on the upper
crust, press down the edges, trim, make several per-
forations in the top to allow the steam to escape,
brush the crust with a little milk, and bake about
forty-five minutes.

RHUBARB PIE

Pie paste.
Rhubarb, 4 cups.
Sugar, 1 large cup.
Nutmeg.
Salt.
Flour.

Line a pie plate with paste rolled a little thicker
than a dollar. Strip the skin off the rhubarb and
cut the stalk into half-inch lengths. Fill the plate
an inch deep, and to a quart of rhubarb add a large
cup of sugar. Sprinkle a pinch of salt, and a grat-
ing of nutmeg on top, with a little flour. Cover

with a rich crust and bake in a quick oven until the pie loosens from the dish.

BLUEBERRY PIE

Line a pie-pan with pie paste. Put in the berries half an inch deep, and to one quart of berries put a teacup of brown sugar; sift a teaspoonful of flour over, a pinch of salt, and a little grated nutmeg. Cover with the top crust, pressing down the edges tightly. Trim and bake in a good oven forty-five minutes. This pie is the typical berry pie.

CAKE

FROSTING

Egg white, beaten stiff, 1.
Corn starch, 1 teaspoonful.
Powdered sugar. 9 tablespoonfuls.
Lemon or orange juice, 1 teaspoonful.
Mix and beat together.

SUNSHINE CAKE

Egg whites, 6.
Egg yolks, 3.
Sugar, granulated, 1 cup.
Flour, 1 scant cup.
Lemon juice, 2 teaspoonfuls.

Mix and bake as for Favorite Sponge Cake, flavor with

Grated rind of lemon.
Juice of ½ orange.

ORANGE CAKE

If boiled icing flavored with orange is used, the result will be orange cake.

ANGEL CAKE

Flour, 1 cup sifted 5 times.
Lemon juice, 2 teaspoonfuls.
Powdered sugar, sifted, 1 cup.
Egg whites, 11 beaten to stiff froth.
Vanilla, 2 teaspoonfuls.

Stir the sugar into the whites very lightly and carefully, adding the vanilla, after which add the flour, stirring quickly and lightly. Pour into a bright, clean cake dish, which should not be buttered or lined. Bake at once in a moderate oven about forty minutes. Test it with a broom splint. When done, let it remain in the cake tin, turning it upside down, with the sides resting on two saucers, so that a current of air will pass over and under it.

SPONGE SHEET

Use and make the ingredients the same as for Simple Sponge Cake, but bake in a sheet. Before baking, sprinkle a generous quantity of the following mixture on top:—

Mix an equal quantity of granulated sugar and chopped almonds and add a small pinch of ground cinnamon. This produces a delicious crust. Bake in a buttered and floured pan, and remove from the pan as soon as done.

SIMPLE SPONGE CAKE

Eggs, 6.
Sifted granulated sugar, 1 cup.
Flour, 1 scant cup.

To the eggs add sugar, and beat with a wire egg beater till the mixture is thick and light colored. Then add the flour, folding it in gently. Drop by the spoonful in an unbuttered pan, and bake in a moderate oven. When done, invert the pan, letting it rest on cups till the cake is cool, when it can easily be taken out. Thus suspended from the bottom of the pan, the cake is stretched by its own weight, which makes it lighter and more elastic than if left to fall by its weight in cooling. The quantity given will make a small loaf cake, or two layers.

FAVORITE SPONGE CAKE

Eggs, 6.
Granulated sugar, 1 cup.
Flour, 1 scant cup.
Lemon juice, 2 teaspoonfuls.

Sift the flour and sugar four or five times. Beat the whites of the egg to a stiff froth, adding the lemon juice. When half beaten, fold in carefully in regular order the sugar, well-beaten yolks of eggs, and the flour. Bake in a moderate oven.

NUT SPONGE CAKE

Eggs, 7.
Water, ¼ cup.
Lemon extract, ¼ teaspoonful.
Ground English walnut, ¾ cup.
Sugar, 1¼ cups.
Vanilla, 1 teaspoonful.
Flour, 1 rounded cup.

Beat the yolks of the eggs till thick; boil sugar in water till it spins a thread. Pour this into the yolks, beating all the time till cool. Add the vanilla and lemon extract; mix flour with walnuts; mix all together, and lastly stir in the stiffly-beaten whites. Bake in tins lined with greased paper.

MARGUERITES

Egg white, 1, partly beaten.
Sugar, 2 tablespoonfuls.
Chopped walnuts, ½ cup.

Stir together and spread on crackers, one inch wide by three or four inches long. Bake a light brown.

SPONGE JELLY CAKE

Eggs, 5.
Lemons, 1.
Sugar, 1 cup.
Flour, 1 cup.

Beat the yolks till very thick, add sugar gradually, then the grated rind and two tablespoonfuls of lemon juice. Fold in one-half of the whites of the eggs, beaten very stiff, then one-half of the flour. the other half of the whites, lastly the remainder of the flour. Bake in a large dripping-pan fifteen minutes. Turn onto a cloth, trim the edges, spread the jelly, and roll up. Wrap in the cloth and set aside to cool.

ALMOND MACAROONS

Egg whites, 5.
Rind of 1 lemon.
Almond meal, 1 scant cup.
Sugar, 2 cups.
Flour, 1 cup.

Beat eggs stiff, add sugar, and beat very stiff; add lemon rind grated; mix and add flour and almond meal. Drop on oiled pans in pieces the size of a walnut, allowing plenty of room between each. Smooth with a knife dipped in water. Bake a light brown.

NUT BUTTER

NUT BUTTER

Nut butter can be easily made in the home, but nearly all the prepared nut foods on sale require expensive machinery and a steam plant to produce, hence can not be made in the home.

Peanuts and almonds are the nuts most suitable for making nut butter. The other varieties are difficult to blanch and do not make good butter. The best variety of peanuts for making nut butter is the Spanish shelled. They are the most easily blanched. Removing the skins from the nuts after they are shelled is called blanching. Peanuts can not be blanched unless they have been thoroughly heated.

To properly cook peanuts is the essential thing to produce a healthful, palatable nut butter. This can be accomplished if care is exercised. There are three ways of cooking them: namely, baking or roasting, boiling, and steaming. The baking process is the easiest way, but care should be used not to scorch them. Scorched or burnt peanuts are unfit to use in any form.

PROCESS NO. 1

Put a layer of peanuts about one-half inch deep in a dripping-pan and place on perforated shelf in a moderate oven. Allow them to bake slowly for about one hour. Cook them until they are a light brown or straw color. Shake the pan or stir the peanuts every few minutes. When the kernels be-

16

gin to crack and pop they brown very quickly and should be watched closely.

A splendid way to cook them is to fill a tight-covered dish about two-thirds full, place in the oven, and shake occasionally. When cooked this way, they are not so liable to burn, and they retain their flavor better. When they have cooked sufficiently, spread out at once. When they have become quite cool, blanch as follows: This can be done by rubbing them in the hands, or what is better, a coarse bag, or take a piece of cloth and fold the ends together, forming a bag. Another good device is a screen made of coarse wire. Rub them until the skins are loose. The chaff can be removed by using a fan or by pouring them from one dish to another where the wind is blowing. Look them over carefully, removing defective nuts and foreign substances.

The next step is to grind them. The most practical family mill we know of for grinding nuts, etc., is the Quaker City Mill (see cut and description of same in this book).

Always grind freshly cooked nuts, as they do not make good butter when left a day or two after being cooked.

PROCESS NO. 2

Thoroughly heat the nuts in an oven, but do not let them brown. Allow them to cool, then blanch as described in process No. 1. Boil them from three to four hours, until they are tender. Drain, spread out on tins, and thoroughly dry them; then grind them through the mill.

PROCESS NO. 3

Heat and blanch the same as for No. 2. Grind them through a meat chopper or the nut butter mill loosely adjusted. Then cook them in a steam cooker about four hours. When tender, drain, spread on tins, and thoroughly dry them. Then run them through the mill tightly adjusted.

SALTED NUT BUTTER

Prepare nuts as described in process No. 1. Sprinkle salt on the kernels when grinding. It is much more preferable to grind the salt in with the nuts than to mix it in the butter.

ALMOND BUTTER

Almond butter is more diffcult to make than peanut butter, on account of the difficulty in removing the skins. Dry heat does not loosen the skins as it does the peanut. To blanch almonds, soak them in boiling water from two to five minutes; then the skins become loose and can be pinched off by pressing on the nut with the thumb and finger; the skins will crack and the kernel pop out. Dry them in a slow oven until they become thoroughly dry and crisp, taking care not to burn them. Then grind them through a loosely adjusted mill. Place on tins or on a cloth stretched over the stove until perfectly dry. Then grind then in the nut butter mill tightly adjusted.

This makes excellent butter if the almonds are first-class and sweet.

BRAZIL NUT BUTTER

Remove the brown, woody skins with a sharp knife and put the nuts through the mill. They may have to be broken up before they can be ground. This butter is very good, but somewhat expensive. It is cheaper to buy the nuts already shelled.

PEANUT MEAL

Heat the peanuts sufficiently to remove the skins, but do not brown them. Blanch and look over. Boil or steam them until tender, taking care to have them quite dry when done. Drain off all the water possible and put them through a colander. Put on tins suspended over the stove, or in a slow oven, with the door open, taking care not to brown them. When prefectly dry and hard, grind through the mill loosely adjusted. If it is not fine enough, spread out to dry some more, pass through the mill again more tightly adjusted, but if the mill is too tight, it will grind it into butter. A good plan is to rub it through a flour sieve.

NUT BUTTER FOR THE TABLE

Put one-half the amount of butter required for the meal into a bowl and dilute with an equal quantity of water, adding a little of the water at a time, beating it thoroughly with a fork until it is smooth and light. Enough water should be used to make it the proper consistency to spread nicely. An egg beater or wire potato masher is an excellent utensil for mixing. A little salt can be added if desired. Nut butter when mixed with water does not keep but a few hours.

PEANUT CREAM

Cook the peanuts until they just begin to turn brown. Then make into butter, ground as fine as possible. Emulsify with water until it is the consistency of milk. Then put in double boiler and cook until it has become as thick as ordinary cream. A little salt can be added if desired. Serve it hot or cold as preferred. It can be made into milk by adding a little water.

VEGETARIAN DIRECTORY

VEGETARIAN RESTAURANTS AND CAFES

VEGETARIAN CAFE, 755 Market Street, San Francisco, Cal.

VEGETARIAN RESTAURANT, 44 San Pablo Avenue, Oakland, Cal.

VEGETARIAN RESTAURANT, 317 West Third Street, Los Angeles, Cal.

GOOD HEALTH RESTAURANT, 616 Third Street, Seattle, Wash.

VEGETARIAN RESTAURANT, 283 Pitt Street, Sydney, N. S. W.

VEGETARIAN RESTAURANT, 54 Farrar Street, Detroit, Mich.

VEGETARIAN RESTAURANT, 607 Locust Street, Des Moines, Ia.

HYGEIA DINING ROOMS, Fifty-eighth Street and Drexel Avenue, Chicago, Ill.

VEGETARIAN RESTAURANT, 145 South Thirteenth Street, Lincoln, Neb.

VEGETARIAN RESTAURANT, Lovstrode 8, Copenhagen, K., Denmark.

VEGETARIAN CAFE, 1543 Glenarm Street, Denver, Colo.

VEGETARIAN CAFE, 322½ North Tejon Street, Colorado Springs, Colo.

THE HYGEIA, Washington Avenue, Battle Creek, Mich.

HYGIENIC CAFE, 1017 Walnut Street, Philadelphia, Pa.

VEGETARIAN RESTAURANT, 170 South Howard Street, Spokane, Wash.

HYGIENIC RESTAURANT, Sheridan, Wyo.

HYGIENIC CAFE, 164 Wisconsin Street, Milwaukee, Wis.

HYGIENIC CAFE, 426 State Street, Madison, Wis.

PURE FOOD CAFE, 410 East Twelfth Street, Kansas City, Mo.

NORTH MICHIGAN TRACT SOCIETY, Petoskey, Mich.

VEGETARIAN RESTAURANT, Corner Church and Vine Street, Nashville, Tenn.

VEGETARIAN RESTAURANT, 105 East Third Street, Jamestown, N. Y.

THE LAUREL, 11 West Eighteenth Street, New York City.

HEALTH RESTAURANT, 391 Sixth Avenue, New York City.

HYGIENIC DINING ROOMS, 1209 G Street, N. W. Washington, D. C.

RESTAURANT, 307 Madison Street, Fairmont, W. Va.

THE PURE FOOD CAFE, 13 South Main Street, Salt Lake City, Utah.

DIRECTORY OF SANITARIUMS

BATTLE CREEK SANITARIUM, Battle Creek, Mich.

CHICAGO SANITARIUM, 28 Thirty-third Place, Chicago, Ill.

PACIFIC UNION MEDICAL MISSIONARY AND BENEVOLENT ASSO-
CIATION, Room 203, Parrott Building, 825 Market Street,
San Francisco, Cal.

ST. HELENA SANITARIUM, Sanitarium, Napa County, Cal.

SAN FRANCISCO BRANCH SANITARIUM, 1436 Market Street,
San Francisco, Cal.

SACRAMENTO TREATMENT ROOMS, 719½ K Street, Sacramento,
Cal.

EUREKA BRANCH SANITARIUM, Corner Third and J Streets,
Eureka, Cal.

SAN FRANCISCO HYDRIATIC DISPENSARY, 916 Laguna Street,
San Francisco, Cal.

PORTLAND SANITARIUM, West Avenue, Mt. Tabor, Ore.

VANCOUVER TREATMENT ROOMS, 338 Columbia Street, Vancouver, B. C.

VICTORIA TREATMENT ROOMS, Victoria, B. C.

PASADENA SANITARIUM, 317 West Third Street, Los Angeles,
Cal.

ARIZONA SANITARIUM, Phoenix, Ariz.

SPOKANE SANITARIUM, Spokane, Wash.

COLLEGE PLACE TREATMENT ROOMS, College Place, Wash.

SAN DIEGO TREATMENT ROOMS, Sefton Block, San Diego, Cal.

TACOMA SANITARIUM, 1016 Tacoma Avenue, Tacoma, Wash.

SEATTLE SANITARIUM, 612 Third Avenue, Seattle, Wash.

WHATCOM SANITARIUM, 1016 Elk Street, Whatcom, Wash.

COLORADO SANITARIUM, Boulder, Colo.

IOWA SANITARIUM, 603 East Twelfth Street, Des Moines, Ia.

NEBRASKA SANITARIUM, College View, Neb.

NEW ENGLAND SANITARIUM, Melrose, Mass.

SOUTHERN SANITARIUM, Graysville, Tenn.

KEENE SANITARIUM, Keene, Tex.

PHILADELPHIA SANITARIUM, 1809 Wallace Street, Philadelphia, Pa.

MADISON SANITARIUM, R. F. D. No. 4, Madison, Wis.

DETROIT SANITARIUM, 54 Farrar Street, Detroit, Mich.

JACKSON SANITARIUM, 106 First Street, Jackson, Mich.

BUFFALO SANITARIUM, 922 Niagara Street, Buffalo, N. Y.

THE TRI-CITY SANITARIUM, 1213 Fifteenth Street, Moline, Ill.

PEORIA SANITARIUM, 203 Third Avenue, Peoria, Ill.

LITTLE ROCK SANITARIUM, 1623 Broadway, Little Rock, Ark.

NASHVILLE SANITARIUM ASSOCIATION, Nashville, Tenn.

PIEDMONT VALLEY SANITARIUM, Hildebran, N. C.

ST. LOUIS SANITARIUM, Fifty-fifth Street and Cabanne Avenue, St. Louis, Mo.

KNOWLTON SANITARIUM, Knowlton, Quebec.

NEWFOUNDLAND SANITARIUM, 282 Duckworth Street, St. Johns, Newfoundland.

CATERHAM SANITARIUM, Caterham, Surrey, England.

LEICESTER SANITARIUM, 80 Regent Street, Leicester, England.

BELFAST SANITARIUM, 39 Antrim Road. Belfast, Ireland.

FRIEDENSAU SANITARIUM, Friedensau, Post Grabow, Bez. Magdeburg. Germany.

INSTITUT SANITAIRE, Weiherweg 48, Basle, Switzerland.

NORWEGIAN PHILANTHROPIC SOCIETY, Akersgaden 74, Christiania, Norway.

SKODSBORG SANATORIUM, Skodsborg, Denmark.

FRYDENSTRANDS SANITARIUM, Frederikshavn, Denmark.

OREBRO HEALTH HOME, Klostergaten 33, Orebro. Sweden.

CAPE SANITARIUM, Plumstead, Cape Colony, South Africa.

SYDNEY SANITARIUM, Wahroonga, N. S. W., Australia.

AVONDALE HEALTH RETREAT, Cooranbong, N. S. W., Australia.

CHRISTCHURCH SANITARIUM, Papanui, Christchurch, New Zealand.

SAMOA SANITARIUM, Apia, Samoa.

GUADALAJARA SANITARIUM, Guadalajara, Mexico.

CALCUTTA SANITARIUM, 51 Park Street, Calcutta, India.

JAPANESE SANITARIUM, 42 Yamamoto-dori, Nichome, Kobe, Japan.

WASHINGTON SANITARIUM, 222 North Capitol Street, Washington, D. C.

DIRECTORY OF SANITARIUM FOOD FACTORIES

BATTLE CREEK SANITARIUM FOOD COMPANY, Battle Creek, Mich.

SANITARIUM FOOD COMPANY, Sanitarium, Cal.

PORTLAND SANITARIUM FOOD COMPANY, West Avenue, Mt. Tabor, Ore.

COLORADO SANITARIUM FOOD COMPANY, Boulder, Colo.

SANITARIUM FOOD COMPANY, 228 Clarence Street, Sydney, N. S. W., Australia.

UNION COLLEGE BAKERY, College View, Neb.

INDEX

17

VEGETABLES—*Continued*